CHOOSING A COLLEGE

Other Books by Ronald Nash

Faith and Reason: Searching for a Rational Faith
Evangelicals in America
Evangelical Renewal in the Mainline Denominations (editor)
Poverty and Wealth: The Christian Debate Over Capitalism
Process Theology (editor)
Liberation Theology (editor)
Christianity and the Hellenistic World
Christian Faith and Historical Understanding
The Concept of God
The Word of God and the Mind of Man
Social Justice and the Christian Church
Freedom, Justice and the State
The Light of the Mind: St. Augustine's Theory of Knowledge
Ideas of History (editor)

The Christian Parent and Student Guide to
CHOOSING A COLLEGE

Ronald H. Nash

Wolgemuth & Hyatt, Publishers
Brentwood, Tennessee

Wolgemuth & Hyatt, Publishers, Inc. is a commercial information packager whose mission is to publish and distribute books that lead individuals toward:

- A personal faith in the one true God: Father, Son, and Holy Spirit;
- A lifestyle of practical discipleship; and
- A worldview that is consistent with the historic, Christian faith.

Moreover, the company endeavors to accomplish this mission at a reasonable profit and in a manner which glorifies God and serves His Kingdom.

Copyright © 1989 by Ronald H. Nash

No part of this publication may be reproduced, stored in a retrieval system, or transmitted in any form by any means, electronic, mechanical, photocopy, recording, or otherwise, without the prior written permission of the publisher, except for brief quotations in critical reviews or articles.

All Scripture quotations are from The Holy Bible: New International Version. Copyright © 1973, 1978, 1984 International Bible Society. Used by permission of Zondervan Bible Publishers.

Wolgemuth & Hyatt, Publishers, Inc.
P.O. Box 1941, Brentwood, Tennessee 37027

Printed in the United States of America

Library of Congress Cataloging-in-Publication Data

Nash, Ronald H.
    Choosing a college / Ronald Nash.
    p. cm.
    Bibliography: p.
    ISBN 0-943497-56-6
    1. College, Choice of—United States. 2. Church colleges—United States. I. Title II. Title: Choosing a college.
LB2350.5.N27   1989
378'.198—dc19   89-5413
                                                       CIP

To
Judith and Emily Newland
whose college years are just beginning

CONTENTS

1. Is This Book Necessary?   1
2. A Chapter Just for Parents   5
3. Five Questions   23
4. Preparing a List of Schools   33
5. How to Reduce Your List of Colleges   43
6. Nonevangelical Colleges   57
7. Evangelical Christian Colleges   71
8. The Effect of Higher Education on Religious Faith   89
9. Some Things to Prepare For   101
10. A Chapter Just for Students   119
    Appendix   127
    Notes   143
    For Further Reading   148
    About the Author   151

ONE

IS THIS BOOK NECESSARY?

Because of all that it involves, the choice of a college is one of life's most important—and most expensive—decisions. The total bill for sending one or more children through college is often, next to the cost of a home, the biggest financial challenge families face. In spite of this, it is a decision many families make more on the basis of guesswork and intuition than on solid information and sound principles.

I have written this book for high school students, who will soon be involved in the vitally important matter of choosing where they'll go to college. This is also a book for the parents of these students, who often find this process surrounded by great confusion, uncertainty, and anxiety. I believe the book will help both students and parents find their way more easily through the complex maze of problems and questions connected with the choice of a college.

The subtitle of the book states that this is a guide for *Christian* parents and students. Christian families understandably have concerns that secular books in this area do not address. They have questions that high school counselors often are not equipped to answer. Where then can they turn for competent advice, not simply on all the usual issues that any family can have, but, more specifically, on the particular kinds of things that might interest only a Christian family?

Suppose your family could invite a qualified person into your home for an evening to discuss the whole matter of choosing a college. Suppose further that this guest is also a Christian who shares the interests and concerns that you as a Christian family have. In an important sense, this scenario is a picture of how I view my task in this book.

The choice of a college is an extremely personal matter. Every family that uses this book is different in important ways. While a particular college might be a good choice for one person, it could be totally wrong for someone else. This is not the kind of situation where someone can feed a lot of information into a personal computer, punch a button, and then receive the name of the right college. For that reason, I make no attempt to recommend any specific school.

What I have done, however, is suggest a procedure that your particular family—with its unique background, values, and goals—can use in arriving at a decision. The decision is yours. My task is providing information and suggestions that will enhance the chances of your decision being right for you.

You have a right to know a little bit about the author of this book. Who is he? Is there good reason to think he knows what he's talking about? Well, for one thing I have been a college professor and administrator for about thirty years. For twenty-five of those years, I have worked for a large state university. But I also taught philosophy and religion in two Christian liberal arts colleges. I received my bachelor's degree from a Christian college. I then moved on to one of the Ivy League universities, where I earned a Master of Arts degree, and finished up with a Doctor of Philosophy degree from Syracuse University. During my many years as both a teacher and an administrator in my state university, I have counseled hundreds of students. I have seen them their first day on campus, when I looked at their scores on the American College Test (ACT) and formed an opinion of how I thought they'd do. I have followed such students through their college years and found how often they surprised me—students with good potential falling by the wayside and others with only average potential excelling. I have taught more than five thousand students over these years. During this period, I've presented lectures at more than fifty colleges and made personal inspections of many others, one of them as head of a team sent by one of the regional accrediting associations.

And so, I'm an educator. Like many in this business, I care about the students I work with. I hate to see young people make wrong decisions. I am interested in helping them get a better education. Obviously, one necessary step in this process is making certain that the first step—the one in which the student chooses his or her college—is the best one for that person.

I am also a parent who has already gone through this process with his own children. My son and daughter have been out of college for a few years now. My wife and I are satisfied with the education our children received; we think our kids made the right decision for them. But, because our family went through this process twice, I can empathize with other parents who are just approaching this mountain. However, I want to do more than empathize; I believe I can also provide some help for these parents.

Finally, I am a Christian. As a Christian, I'm concerned about the future of the Christian Church, which rests to a large extent on the minds, hearts, and hands of its young people. Wrong choices about higher education have led many Christians to reject their faith. Many others have failed to reach their potential because the college they selected failed them in important respects.

While this book covers a lot of topics, its core concerns a procedure a family can use as it moves from a situation where it first has no idea what colleges to consider, to one where it has a list of schools it is actively considering, to the point, finally, where it is in a position to put one college at the top of its list. I suggest ways of identifying colleges that you will want to look into more carefully. I also discuss how to get information you'll need to evaluate and rank these schools. I outline the advantages and disadvantages of attending a Christian college over against a secular university.

The next chapter in the book is intended just for parents. Since it contains no secrets, I have no objection to students' reading it. I simply felt that I had to begin the book by discussing a number of subjects that would be of interest primarily to parents. My advice to the student reader is to skip the next chapter and move directly to chapter three. If it's any consolation, the very last chapter in the book is directed exclusively to the student.

One other thing before I start. I have decided to use a few footnotes. One reason for using them is because it's impossible to get very far in college without encountering them. Students reading the book can regard the footnotes as a kind of bonus, a painless introduction to one of college's little necessities. The more important reason for using footnotes is because they enable me to do some important things that a book like this should do. Sometimes I need to make important comments that would otherwise interrupt the flow of the main discussion. On other occasions, I use footnotes to identify the source of quotations. Finally, I use some footnotes to direct the reader to other books he or she should consider reading. Having said all this, I've made an important concession to all those readers who find footnotes intimidating in some way. I've tucked them away in the back of the book where they can be ignored by anyone who wants to pretend they aren't there.

TWO

A CHAPTER JUST FOR PARENTS

I tried to avoid writing this chapter but couldn't. Then I tried putting it somewhere else in the book but couldn't. I finally decided that there were a number of things I had to say to parents and that I had to say them at the beginning of the book.

I'm not sure there is any single thread that ties the subjects of this chapter together. They do contribute, in a way, to helping us all get started at the same place. If some later chapters are analogous to setting the table before everyone sits down to eat, this chapter can be viewed as akin to putting the legs on the table and straightening up the room.

I begin the chapter by noting something that should be obvious: the tremendous variety that will be found among the families using this book. If it's important that we all get as close as possible to the same starting point, it is worthwhile pointing out some of the factors that place us in different relationships to that point. I then move to an explanation of how I use the word *Christian* throughout the book. Because this word unfortunately is used in so many different ways, there is value in clarifying what I mean by the term. Then I argue that Christian families have a right to make important values and beliefs a factor in their choice of a college. Following this, I point out that parental concern for children functions on a number of different levels, all of which are important. Unfortunately, many parents are never able to move beyond one or two of these levels. In some cases, this happens because no one has ever told them that parental concern has these other dimensions. Perhaps my discussion will help more fathers and mothers advance to levels that will result not only in a wiser choice of a college, but also in their being able to provide more support for their child while he or she is in college. The chapter concludes with some suggestions about ways in which concerned parents can help their children get an early start in areas that will help them through the college years.

Family Differences

Every family using this book is different. Individuals within families vary in their religious commitment. A wife may take her Christianity more seriously than her husband, for example. One or more members of the family may not be Christian. Families also differ in the extent to which they understand important doctrines of the Christian faith. Some families know the Bible better, understand Christianity better, have a better grasp of their culture along with the various conflicts between that culture and the Christian faith. Some families read more widely than others. Some have a longer history of contact with higher education.

In some families, the parents are committed believers, while the child may be lukewarm toward the faith and lack interest in important religious, spiritual, and moral issues. In other families, it is the young person whose commitment to Christ stands out, and it is the parents who may be indifferent to Christianity. Some parents and young people see college only in terms of how it will contribute to the student's worldly success. In other cases, there is more concern that the student leave college as a committed believer trained to take whatever place God has for him or her in the world.

All these variables pose a challenge for anyone writing a book on this subject. Ideally, I would like to assume that every parent and student will start the journey from exactly the same starting point. That is, each is a faithful, practicing Christian who knows the Bible well, who is familiar with contemporary challenges to the Christian faith, who understands the importance of higher education regardless of what kind of vocation is planned, but who also recognizes that the purpose of a college degree is to help the Christian better discharge his or her responsibility to God in life.

If this book ends up in homes where members of the family are not Christians, don't know the Bible or the doctrines of Christianity as well as they should, don't pay attention to what's going on in the world, don't read serious books, ignore the development of their mind as well as their spirit, or care little about putting God and His kingdom first, I hope that some of the things I say will lead them to begin addressing these problems. But this particular book has other issues to discuss.

The Meaning of the Word *Christian*

This book is offered as a guide to Christian parents and students. Because the word *Christian* means so many different things to people, it's necessary that I spend a little time explaining how the term is used in this book.

The word *Christian* is sometimes understood to mean any person born in the United States who is neither an atheist nor a member of some non-Christian religion. Such a broad, indiscriminate use of the term is inconsistent with the New Testament and effectively deprives the word of any significance.

The Christian audience I have in view in this book is that

group of theologically conservative Protestants who have made a personal commitment to Jesus Christ. They are also people who view the Bible as God's inspired revelation and treat it as their basic rule of faith and practice. People like this are often—at least in the United States—called evangelicals.[1] In short then, I am writing this book for people who live within the rather large religious family known as American evangelicalism. If estimates I have seen are correct, there are around fifty million such evangelicals in America.

If they are properly informed, all members of the larger evangelical family share a number of core beliefs. For example, they believe in the doctrine of the Trinity. As the Apostles' Creed states, "I believe in God the Father Almighty . . . and in Jesus Christ his only Son our Lord . . . [and] in the Holy Spirit." As one consequence of this, they believe in the deity of Jesus Christ; Jesus Christ was not simply a human being. Nor is it correct to say simply that Jesus was like God. All orthodox Christians affirm that Jesus Christ is God. Evangelical Christians use the word *incarnation* to express their belief that the birth of Jesus Christ marked the entrance of the eternal and divine Son of God into the human race. Orthodox Christians also believe that Jesus entered this world expressly to die. The purpose of His death was to make things right between the Holy God and sinful humans who, because of sin, are separated from God. Jesus' death was neither an accident nor an act of martyrdom. He died as a sacrifice for human sins. It is important, evangelicals insist, that human beings realize that Christ died for each one of us. He took the punishment that every human being deserves. He died in our place. Evangelical Christians also believe in the resurrection of Christ, the central event of the New Testament. Such people recognize further the human need for forgiveness and redemption and stress that the blessings of salvation are possible only because of Jesus' death and resurrection. Evangelicals note the importance that Jesus Himself placed upon conversion when He said: "I tell you the truth, unless you change [are converted] and become like little children, you will never enter the kingdom of heaven" (Matthew 18:3). Christ's redemptive work is the ground, or basis, of human salvation. But human beings are required to repent (be sorry) of their sins and believe. Accepting Christ as one's Lord and Savior brings about a new birth, a new heart, a new relation to God, and a new power to live (see John 3:3–21; Hebrews 8:10–12; 1 John 3:1–2; and Galatians 2:20). Orthodox Christians also believe the Apostles' Creed when it states that Christ shall come from heaven "to judge the quick [living] and the dead." These are just some of the central, or core, beliefs shared by all knowledgeable evangelical Christians.

This core of evangelical beliefs is challenged today from many directions. It is opposed by atheism that denies the existence of God, by naturalism that regards this world as the only reality that exists, by humanism that glorifies man as the ultimate source of value in the universe, as well as by various kinds of non-Christian religions and religious substitutes, such as the New Age movement.

It is unfortunate that so many Christians possess such a weak understanding of their own religion; they are often unable to explain to themselves or to others exactly *what* Christians are supposed to believe. It is also cause for concern when Christians lack the ability to answer challenges from those who seek to deny Christianity its rightful place in the marketplace of ideas.

A Question of Values

Families have every right to choose a college that they believe will support values important to them. To knowingly select a college that regularly attacks or undermines such values without solid, overriding reasons would be foolish and irresponsible.

Whenever we choose thoughtfully, we rank things according to their importance to us and choose those options that offer us more of the things that matter most to us. Readers not part of the wider Christian family for whom this book is intended may not share some of the values that should be part of the decision-making process for evangelical parents and students. But such non-Christians ought to be able to appreciate the fact that Christian families have a right to make choices consistent with and supportive of their values. Within a free society, that is their privilege. Within the Christian family, that is their duty. Hence, it is perfectly proper for Christian families to appraise educational institutions in terms of these values.

Some of these values are obviously going to be religious in nature. How could it be otherwise for *Christian* families? Christian parents understandably take their belief system seriously and want their children to share those beliefs.

In the previous section of this chapter, I identified a number of beliefs that should be important to *all* who are Christians in the New Testament sense of the word. But some Christians also get excited about less central—or more debatable—issues. That is, they take certain beliefs and practices as important, when others within the larger family of evangelicalism disagree.

Some of these differences are the sorts of things that divide us denominationally. I have no interest in this book in trying to settle such disagreements. I mention them here because I believe that the kinds of things that make some of us Methodists, Baptists, Lutherans, or Presbyterians are also legitimate factors to consider when choosing a college. If certain denominational distinctives are important to your family, then they are something you'll want to consider as this book proceeds. My point here is simply to draw attention to such values and acknowledge their relevance. If it is important to your family that your child attend a college related to your denomination, or one which supports beliefs and practices associated with your denomination, it is my contention that this is both your privilege and your right. You'll not find me criticizing thinking along these lines.

Christians disagree over many things: Some of us are Calvinists, while others are Arminians.[2] Some are Pentecostal or charismatic, while others are not. Some are dispensationalist,[3] while others are not. When families feel strongly enough about these matters, they might decide to avoid a college where such a belief is treated unsympathetically. This is not a practice I necessarily recommend; I simply see nothing wrong with it. I am doing nothing more in this paragraph than noting for the record that when a Methodist or Calvinistic or charismatic family finds themselves leaning toward a college that they know will treat their convictions sympathetically, their action is both understandable and proper. Of course, other families with the same convictions may recognize that these issues are less central than the core of Christian beliefs noted earlier. And so these families may decide in favor of a college that may represent a different stance on nonessential issues.

Christians also disagree on issues that seem less directly related to biblical or doctrinal matters. Some of these differences spill over into the social and political arena. For example, some churches are pacifist, while others believe the Bible recognizes the possibility of so-called just wars. A family that has a low opinion of political conservatism would probably decide against sending their child to Jerry Falwell's Liberty University or to the graduate school at Pat Robertson's CBN University, both of which, incidentally, are fine institutions. On the other hand, a politically conservative Christian family might think twice about sending their child to one of the growing number of evangelical colleges exhibiting a bias toward political liberalism, providing the family knows about this bias. While the conservative bent of Liberty University is common knowledge, the liberal bias at many highly regarded evangelical colleges is seldom mentioned in public. I'm not sure why this is so, unless the administrators at these colleges fear it might hurt their recruitment of students.

To summarize this section, I think it is perfectly proper for Christian families to take the kinds of values and beliefs I've described into account when they are involved in choosing a college.

Levels of Parental Concern

Parental concern for children functions on several different levels. Where parents stand on this ladder of concern will affect the quality of their influence on the decision-making process I'm dealing with in this book.

The Level of Emotional Concern

The first and most basic level of parental concern is emotional. I guess this is where all of us who are parents begin; we all regard any parent lacking this level of concern as abnormal. We love our children; we care what happens to them; we want the best for them.

There is nothing wrong with this level of parental concern for one's children. The problem arises when parents' concern for their children fails to go beyond this level. I'm glad that you love your children. I want you now to recognize that your concern for them must function on other levels as well.

The Level of Spiritual Concern

When the level of a parent's concern is limited merely to the emotional, that parent's vision of what is most important for the child will be defective in important ways. Many parents seem incapable of seeing beyond the goal of temporal happiness and success for their children. This happiness is usually linked to "a good job" that includes a salary that will permit them to comfortably satisfy most of their material wants and needs. For such parents, a college education is seen simply as a means to such an end.

The wise Christian parent recognizes that there is more to life than this. God calls His children to live their lives for Him and for others. Parents who reach the level of spiritual concern want more than earthly success and material prosperity for their children. They want their children to be faithful believers who love the Lord and His Word, and who sincerely want to do His will. Some of the major issues at the level of spiritual concern are conversion, Christian living, and Christian service. Of course, the notion of Christian service should always be seen in the broader context of what Martin Luther called the doctrine of Christian vocation. God does not call every Christian into some form of full-time Christian work or ministry. We should thank God for talented young people who decide to prepare for a career in some form of ministry. But, we should also thank God for talented and faithful young people who decide to fulfill their Christian vocation as farmers, teachers, businesspeople, and auto mechanics.

The Level of Theological Concern

I have never met a genuine Christian who disparaged the importance of conversion, faith, commitment, sacrifice, Bible study, holy living, and the like. But I know lots of Christians who have not yet seen the importance of sound doctrine. It is important *that* we believe (spiritual concern), but it is also important *what* we believe (theological concern).

More than eighty years ago, a great Scottish theologian named James Orr puzzled over Christians who treat the doctrinal element of Christianity as unimportant. "If there is a religion in the world which exalts the office of teaching," he wrote, "it is safe to say that it is the religion of Jesus Christ."[4] While doctrine is unimportant in most pagan religions, Orr continued, "this is precisely where Christianity distinguishes itself from other religions—it does contain doctrine. It comes to men with definite, positive teaching; it claims to be the truth; it bases religion on knowledge, through a knowledge which is only attainable under moral conditions."[5] Orr was amazed that any discerning Christian could be uncertain about the importance of doctrine for Christianity. "A religion based on mere feeling is the vaguest, most unreliable, most unstable of all things. A strong, stable, religious life can be built upon no other ground than that of intelligent conviction. . . . Christianity, therefore, addresses itself to the intelligence as well as to the heart."[6]

There are segments of Christianity that appear to stress *only* doctrine or creeds; they appear to say that the only important thing is believing the correct propositions. In the process of doing this, some of these denominations fail to tell people that there is a personal and subjective side to the Christian faith. We must believe the right truths; but we must also believe *in* the right *person*, Jesus Christ! What we know objectively must be combined with a genuine subjective commitment.

But there are also elements of the Christian Church that emphasize only the subjective or inner side of Christian faith to the neglect of the objective, theological side. Whenever this happens, Christians are operating with something less than the full Gospel.

In my work as a theologian, I am very familiar with a large American denomination that, for years, tended to ignore the level of theological concern I've just described. Most of the church members in this denomination claim to have had the religious experience called conversion; they have been properly concerned about holy living, prayer, and Christian experience. But for decades, many of the clergy and laypeople in this denomination ignored the importance of sound doctrine. During those years, some unfortunate things took place in the colleges and seminaries of the denomination. In many of these schools, professors and administrators began to move away from essential Christian beliefs; they took positions that undermined the authority of the Bible. Various types of liberalism became entrenched on some of these campuses. In the meantime, thousands of faithful parents continued to send their children to denominational schools. While at these schools, the beliefs of many of these young people were changed dramatically. Many left their denominational schools with their faith in the Bible and in New Testament Christianity badly weakened. Because the denomination tended to downplay or ignore doctrine, no one, it seemed, paid any attention, while the theological situation in the colleges and seminaries grew even worse. Today, earnest and pious members of that denomination continue to support with their dollars schools that often tear down doctrines that these Christians would clearly defend with their lives—if only they could rise to the level of theological concern. A similar pattern is being followed in a number of American denominations where the people in the churches are more conservative than those who are running the academic institutions. While the faithful church members, who pay the bills, concentrate on their own religious experience, the professors in their denominational colleges and seminaries are tinkering with the theological foundations of the Christian faith.

If your children are to be properly prepared for the years ahead, they should know the objective dimension of their faith; they should understand what they as Christians are supposed to believe. Moreover, they should also be introduced to the good and sound reasons *why* Christians believe these truths. The children of most Christian parents enter college with absolutely no preparation for the challenges to their faith that they'll encounter. They have no idea why they believe that God exists or why Jesus is the Son of God or why the miracle of Christ's resurrection occurred. Suddenly, without any warning, they are confronted by a professor who tells them about the problem of evil. Without any guidance or help, some of them naturally begin to think that perhaps there is no reason for the evil that exists in the world; maybe God isn't all-powerful after all; or perhaps God doesn't really exist. Even worse, when and if they ask their parents about these problems, they discover that their parents don't have any answers either.

Christian parents who have failed to rise to the level of theological concern cannot possibly be ready to provide help for their children in these matters. The first step in getting children prepared theologically for what awaits them is for the parents of those children to prepare themselves. I believe this task is every bit as important as finding the money to pay for your children's education. But it remains a job that practically no Christian parents even begin.

Later in this book, I suggest ways in which theologically concerned parents can prepare first themselves and then their children to meet these theological challenges.

The Level of Intellectual Concern

This is undoubtedly the hardest rung of the ladder to get most Christian parents to climb. All normal parents are emotionally involved with their children, and it is relatively easy to get Christian parents to see that their parental love must be extended to include concern for their children's spiritual well-being. As I've just pointed out, it is harder to get these same parents to recognize the importance of such studies as theology and apologetics. But, even at the level of theological concern, we're dealing with issues that have a clear relevance to the Christian faith. What makes this last level—what I call the level of intellectual concern—so much tougher to achieve is its apparent irrelevance to typical religious concerns. What I'm talking about on this level is knowledge for its own sake: the study of history or mathematics or economics or philosophy or art or music, even when no direct relationship to Christianity is apparent.

One of the biggest obstacles in all this is getting Christian parents (and students) to appreciate the importance of their minds. I wonder how many of my readers have ever noticed that the first and greatest commandment, according to Jesus, requires us to love God with all our heart and all our soul and all our *mind* (see Matthew 22:37). The common Christian practice of compartmentalizing knowledge into sacred and secular is unbiblical and leads to the dangerous notion that secular knowledge is somehow less important, worldly, and hence unfit for the spiritual Christian. Although the truth God has revealed in Scripture is sufficient for faith and conduct, it is not exhaustive. The truth we can find outside the Bible is also important and worthy of our attention and careful study. Even revealed truth requires study and interpretation, tasks that can be aided by an education in such "secular" subjects as philosophy and history.

We must reject the mistaken belief that faith somehow provides the Christian with a shortcut to the truth that eliminates any need for a grounding in so-called secular areas of learning.

During the years of 1987 and 1988, the literary world was shocked to discover that a serious book by a University of Chicago philosopher had become a best-seller. That book, *The Closing of the American Mind* by Allan Bloom, is worthwhile reading for any Christians who might aspire to reach the intellectual level. While it is not a religious book, much that Bloom says about higher education will be appreciated by Christian readers. Take the following as an example. Bloom writes that many modern families "have nothing to give their children in the way of a vision of the world, of high models of action or profound sense of connection with others. . . . The family requires a certain authority and wisdom about the ways of the heavens and of men. The parents must have knowledge of what has happened in the past, and prescriptions for what ought to be, in order to resist the philistinism or the wickedness of the present."[7] In other words, few parents can be any real help to their children in college unless they also have acquired a foundation in certain important areas.

Bloom continues: "People sup together, play together, travel together, but they do not think together. Hardly any homes have any intellectual life whatsoever, let alone one that informs the vital interests of life."[8] Reflect a bit on all the things your family has done together. When was the last time your family spent time thinking together? Christians need to work at developing a Christian mind; and they should do this in partnership with every other member of their family. To seek knowledge is an important part of what it means to be a fully developed Christian.

What this means is simple: If parental concern is functioning on all the proper levels, it will include a concern that children develop mentally as well as spiritually. In order for parents to have the same degree of input on the level of ideas as they might have, say, on the emotional and spiritual level, the parents themselves have got to work at keeping in touch with the contemporary world of ideas.

Most parents are satisfied if they simply get their child admitted to an acceptable college and find, four years later, that things have worked out well. A smaller number of parents will want to be able to answer their children's questions about theological and intellectual matters or at least be ready to recommend books that offer answers. A still smaller group of parents will want to be several steps ahead of their kids, be able to anticipate their questions and lay a foundation for future challenges before the questions are even asked. In the next section of this chapter, I suggest various things parents should consider doing long before the search for a college even begins.

Helping Children Get an Early Start

One reason college students never reach their full potential is because they failed to reach a number of intermediary goals before they entered college. Picture a long-distance runner who wants to be close enough at the finish line to challenge for first place. This runner should know that in order to be in that position at the end of the race, he or she will have to meet certain goals all through the race. The runner may know, for example, that he or she must run the first half of the race within a certain time. Many college freshmen have fallen way behind in important areas of intellectual development.

Every year, I teach about 200 students in an Introduction to Philosophy course (about fifty students in each section of the course). Most of them are freshmen. In addition to teaching the students about philosophy, I use the course as a way of helping them to organize and express ideas in essay form. This is something that contemporary students have not been prepared to do by their high school courses. Recently, however, I have begun to realize that there is another reason why today's college students cannot write decent essays: They simply have not read enough. They cannot spell because they haven't seen most of these words in print; they cannot write decent sentences because the little they learned about grammar hasn't been reinforced by sufficient reading experience; their paragraphs cannot rise above the mundane because their exposure to the vocabulary and writing style of good authors is so limited. And so this brings me to my first recommendation to parents who want to help their children get an early start: Encourage your children to read.

Allan Bloom, whom I quoted earlier, points out that students today "have lost the practice of and the taste for reading. They have not learned how to read, nor do they have the expectation of delight or improvement from reading."[9] The rich, wonderful world of great books is as foreign to most modern students as the American continent was to the pilgrims when they first set foot on this land. They knew something was out there but could only guess as to what it was. The failure to read good books, Bloom continues, "enfeebles the vision and strengthens our most fatal tendency—the belief that the here and now is all there is."[10]

Parents should do everything possible to develop a love for reading in their children. As children reach appropriate levels in their development, they should be encouraged to read quality books suitable for young people with their ability. It is even better when at least one parent reads the book at the same time and is able to discuss it with the child.

In addition to the great classics, children should be motivated to do the kind of reading and thinking that will prepare them to develop theologically. C. S. Lewis is a marvelous resource for this kind of thing. Lewis's children's stories are an especially good way to get children to start thinking about theological subjects, as well as getting them interested in Lewis as a writer. Once they acquire a taste for Lewis, they may eventually be ready to pick up some of his more theological writings such as *Mere Christianity, Miracles,* and *The Problem of Pain.*

Any good reading program must include the Bible. Make sure a good, readable, modern version of the Bible is available. Help your children to see how important a good background in the Bible is for understanding many literary classics. *Moby Dick* can serve well in this regard.

Also, find ways of encouraging your children to read relatively simple books that explain what Christians believe and why they believe this way. One problem here is the shortage of good books that are both intelligible and interesting to high school students. Most Sunday school literature is practically worthless for this purpose. When visiting Christian bookstores, be on the watch for books that are suitable for this task. One such book is Paul Little's *Know Why You Believe*.[11] Admittedly, it takes a special young man or woman (or a specially prepared young person) to read books like this in high school. If one approach fails to produce a voluntary and interested response, drop it and seek for another.

Consider ways of working an educational angle into your family travels. For families that can afford it, foreign travel frequently gets young people excited about new areas of study. A carefully planned trip to Great Britain, for example, can do wonders for a student's interest in history. I remember how interested my own children became in learning more about the history of Great Britain after visiting England. A brief stop at the home of the Brontë sisters in northern England generated an interest in their novels. A two-day stop in Edinburgh, Scotland, produced a desire to know more about John Knox and the Scottish Reformation.

Some parents might complain at this time that I'm confusing them with their children's teachers. Such a response only demonstrates one of the problems of the modern family. Fathers and mothers are the most important teachers their children will ever have. It is the failure of so many modern parents to fulfill this role that is at the root of many students' problems.

Your child's progress in high school should be carefully monitored. Watch her progress in writing courses. Be certain he takes the college preparatory program and skips none of the important courses in English, math, and history.

Some time before your child's junior year in high school, suggest that he or she begin preparing for the college boards that I describe in the next chapter. Most good bookstores carry books that can help students get ready for the SAT and ACT tests. Once you understand these tests yourself, you can explain their importance to your child.

Later chapters in this book explain other ways you can help your child, such as getting literature about colleges you're considering and visiting those schools.

Because of the expense involved, it is never too soon to begin saving the money that will be needed to pay for that college education. Talk to high school counselors about the kind of financial aid that may be available in your state. Begin to gather both dollars and information for the day when you have to write that first check.

I suppose that the most important points in this chapter can be summed up by saying that the most important thing fathers and mothers can do in helping get their children ready for college is for them to work at being good and complete parents.

THREE

FIVE QUESTIONS

My time of talking exclusively to parents is over. Whenever I use the word *you* from this point on, I am speaking to the students in my audience. I am writing for your parents as well, but I'll think of them as though they were reading the rest of the book over your shoulder.

In this chapter, I ask and answer five questions that ought to be considered fairly early in the process of selecting a college. They are: (1) Should you go to college? (2) Is getting into college difficult? (3) When should your preparation begin? (4) What about the SAT and ACT tests? (5) What about the selection process that colleges use to pick their students?

Should You Go to College?

The percentage of high school graduates who go on to college varies greatly, depending on the area of the country. The percentage is higher in suburban high schools than for inner-city schools. It is higher in states like Massachusetts than in states like Kentucky. Many young people who never go to college would have if their high schools had done a better job of preparing them or if their families had done more to motivate, encourage, or push them. And so, there are lots of young people who should go to college but don't.

As an experienced college professor, I can also attest that there are lots of young people who enter college when they shouldn't have. I have had to act as an adviser to many college freshmen who fit this description on their first day in college. It can be very frustrating to see the student's low high school grades and his incredibly bad ACT scores and wonder who talked this young person into entering college.

But the question before us is, should *you* go to college? Without knowing a thing about your high school grades and your SAT/ACT scores, you already have one thing going for you. Someone in your family visits bookstores; I assume they had to in order for this book to have ended up in your home. That in itself is a victory of sorts. Moreover, that person brought home a book titled *Choosing A College*, which says that this is a matter she cares about. And now *you* are actually reading this book. Based on my contact with more than five thousand students, I'm prepared to offer this generalization: If you're interested enough to finish this book and competent enough to understand what it says, you are college material.

Is there anything more scientific to go on? Certainly there is. Your scores on the SAT and/or ACT tests will provide very helpful information. Your high school counselor has been trained in this area. Listen carefully to what she says.

But there is another place to look for an answer: inside yourself! Do *you* want to go? Many of the young people I face each fall are in college because someone else wanted them there, when they would have preferred doing something else. Do you really understand how important a college education can be for you? How badly do you want what college can offer you?

Midway through the 1987 fall semester, I answered a knock on my office door. When I opened the door, I was greeted by a lady who I judged was in her early forties. After sitting down, she told me the following story. "You probably don't remember me," she began. "More than twenty years ago, I was a freshman student in your Introduction to Philosophy class. Early in the semester, I decided to drop out of school and return home. I just wasn't interested in college; perhaps I wasn't ready. Because I didn't care, I didn't even take the trouble to withdraw officially from my classes. Therefore, I got an F in your course."

She went on to explain that after dropping out of school, she had married. Now, more than twenty years later, her children had left home for college, and she had decided to return for the degree she hadn't been ready to pursue. She had now reached the point where she had to remove the F she had gotten in my course from her record. When I asked her what grades she was getting this time around, she replied that she was now a straight A student.

I've told this story because I believe this lady is typical of many college freshmen. The reason they do poorly and eventually drop out is not because they're dumb. What they lack is not intelligence, but maturity, interest, and commitment. Until young people like this acquire that needed inner drive to succeed, they might as well spend their time somewhere else. This inner drive is seldom missing from people who enter college later in life.

If your high school grades are satisfactory and your SAT/ACT scores are acceptable, you have the ability. If you also have the desire, then by all means you should go. The long-range costs of not going to college are so high today that you owe it to yourself at least to give it a try.

Is Getting Into College Difficult?

I'm sure you know that there are a number of colleges and universities that are very hard to get into. If you're one of the exceptionally bright people who has a chance to get into one of the top one hundred colleges in the country, go for it—if that's what you want. Your high school counselor is probably the best person to advise you on this matter. But if you're not in that league or don't care for the status that many people associate with such schools, there are lots of other fine colleges in the country where you can get an excellent education. In fact, most of these schools would probably love to have you as a student. They will recruit you, woo you, and attempt to persuade you that there's no better place on earth for you to pursue your college education.

There are also plenty of American colleges that will admit anyone alive and healthy enough to carry their high school diploma into the admissions office. Many of these schools are reluctant to admit this, of course, and go through the motions of an admissions process. But as long as they have empty dormitory rooms and empty classroom desks, they have what amounts to an open admissions policy. Other schools eliminate only the most hopeless applicants. Some regional state universities have a policy of admitting almost any high school graduate from within their state and applying somewhat higher standards to out-of-state applicants.

So, is getting into college difficult? In the case of the one hundred or so most exclusive schools in the country, the answer is yes. But beyond them, there are many other fine schools that will love to learn that you might be interested in studying on their campus.

When Should You Begin the Search?

A number of modern families start the process of getting their child into college much too early. To take what is perhaps the most extreme kind of case, some parents struggle to get their children into exclusive pre-schools, because this will increase their chances later of getting into exclusive kindergartens, and then exclusive private elementary schools. All of this is seen as a prelude to getting them into an exclusive prep school, which is supposed to open the door to an exclusive college. People like this would be better advised to spend some of this money to secure psychological counseling for themselves. Anyway, it is possible to start the process too early.

It is also possible to begin the process too late. If a student waits until after his or her high school graduation to begin thinking about college, his or her choices will be severely limited—at least for the first year. It can take several months to get all of the paperwork done. If one waits too long, the only option may be a junior college, where the admission process can be completed in a few days.

Probably the best time to begin thinking seriously about college is early in a student's sophomore year in high school. Even then, there is usually little need to think about more than selecting the right high school courses and making sure the student does well in them. Following the high school's college preparatory program should be mandatory.

The big events during the junior year are the taking of the SAT and/or the ACT tests, described in the next section of the chapter. By the end of the junior year, it is wise to have begun work on a list of possible colleges, a process I say more about later in the book. The summer before a student's senior year is a good time to begin collecting college catalogs and possibly visiting a few campuses, although campus visits are best taken when the college is in regular session. Applications should be mailed late in the fall of the senior year, or at least in time to beat whatever deadline is specified in the college catalog. In the case of schools that admit only a small percentage of applicants, an even earlier mailing of admission forms is advisable.

What About The SAT and ACT Tests?

Almost every college in the country utilizes one of these two tests as a factor in evaluating student applications; the college catalog will tell you which one applies in its case. Even if you're unsure about going to college, you should take the tests during your junior year. I recommend taking both tests along with the PSAT (Preliminary Scholastic Aptitude Test) that is offered during the fall of the junior year.

As its name suggests, the Scholastic Aptitude Test (SAT) measures your aptitude or potential for college-level work. The American College Test (ACT) is an achievement test that measures what you already know as well as your ability to use that knowledge. The ACT measures how well you can handle questions in English, mathematics, social studies, and the natural sciences. The SAT provides a measure of your verbal and mathematical competence.

A large number of books are available that are useful in preparing for these exams. They are usually available at better bookstores. They contain sample questions (with answers) that can give you a feel for the test. The practice you'll get from working through such books is a worthwhile investment of time and money.

When your test scores arrive, they'll be accompanied by information that will help you and your family interpret them. Perhaps the quickest way to see how you did is to look at the number identifying the percentile into which your scores fall. Let us suppose that your ACT English score places you in the eightieth percentile. What that means is that of all the students who took the same test at the same time, eighty percent of those students got a lower score than you; only twenty percent did better.

Information like this can be much more helpful than your high school grades. The reason is that high schools, even when located in the same city, can vary greatly in quality. A student with an A average in courses offered by a relatively weak high school might have gotten only C's had he or she studied in a school with higher standards and better teachers. One thing your percentile shows is where you stand relative to all the other students across the nation who took the same test.

But some caution is needed. Scores on these tests are not infallible indicators either of what you know or of your potential. I have known students who flunked out of college after entering school with very promising scores. I have known other students whose scores seemed to predict that they would be only average college students who went on to become A or B students. While these exams can reveal something of the student's past learning, native intelligence, and ability, they cannot measure such things as motivation, determination, commitment, and willingness to work hard.

It is always wise to talk to your high school counselor about your test scores. If the scores are marginal and raise questions about your potential for college, a parent's visit with the counselor should certainly be considered. Students whose scores rank near the bottom should be realistic and begin to look for alternatives to a four-year college.

What About the Selection Process?

Colleges use several of the following factors in deciding which students to admit:
(1) high school grades and rank in high school class
(2) score on the SAT or ACT exam
(3) difficulty of high school courses
(4) recommendations
(5) an application essay (if required)
(6) results of a personal interview with a college official (if required)

(7) extracurricular activities

According to the January 26, 1988, issue of *USA Today*, this ordering of the factors reflects the importance that colleges attach to them; at least, this is what a *USA Today* survey of American colleges revealed. The most important piece of information by far was the student's grades. The SAT/ACT scores were a distant second. Of course, you must remember that the colleges you're interested in may assign a different importance to these factors.

Most evangelical Christian colleges will also want to know about the applicant's religious beliefs and commitment. They may ask you for a statement about your conversion experience. If you don't know what this means or doubt that you've had such an experience, this would be a good time to talk to a parent, pastor, or Christian friend about this important matter. Many Christian schools will also want to know about your personal habits. Some of them frown upon such activities as smoking and use of alcoholic beverages. When this is the case, students are expected to refrain from such activities while a student or at least while on campus. If you disagree with such restrictions and have no intention of complying, you should look elsewhere for a college.

Conclusion

In this chapter, I have looked at five questions that students and parents normally ask near the beginning of the process that will end with their choice of a college. All things being equal, you ought to go through high school assuming that you are going to seek a college degree somewhere. Getting into some college somewhere is not all that difficult; what may be tougher is getting admitted to a specific school that happens to have relatively high admissions standards. Ordinarily, the best time to begin the process of choosing a college is early in your sophomore year in high school. If you're wise, you'll go into your SAT and ACT exams prepared with the help of readily available books. Your scores will reveal much about academic areas where you're weak. They can also provide clues as to how high you should aim in your selection of a college. And finally, you now know how much importance most colleges place upon your high school grades and your ranking in your high school class.

FOUR

PREPARING A LIST OF SCHOOLS

At some stage early in the process, it's a good idea to prepare a working list of colleges that will be getting most of your attention. The list can be as long or as short as you like. Perhaps you'll begin with only one school and, as time passes, add more names to it. Possibly you'll start with ten or more names and pare it down. Certainly, the names on your list will change. But it is wise to focus your attention on a limited number of colleges in this way.

Getting Names for Your List

The major question at this point is determining what schools should go on your working list. How do you learn about colleges you may have never heard of but that might be right for you? How do you discover that a school offers something you're looking for?

Since this book is a guide for Christian parents and students, I hope that every family using it will begin by taking a careful look at the many fine evangelical Christian colleges in the country. Later chapters of this book will discuss the strengths and weaknesses of colleges in this group. For now, you may wish to turn to the appendix at the end of this book where I identify approximately sixty such schools. The colleges are grouped by states. In all but a few cases, the colleges I mention are fully accredited. I mention how many students the college has and what its denominational affiliation or theological emphasis may be. Before your working list is ready, I hope that some of these names will appear on it. For the record, I should note that no effort was made to make my list of evangelical Christian colleges complete. There are schools I do not mention that you may wish to include on your list.

Many evangelical Christian colleges publish ads in religious magazines. If your family subscribes to some of these magazines, study those ads and take note of those that catch your interest. Additional information about the Christian college movement can be found in a directory, *Peterson's Consider a Christian College,* that can be purchased for $12.95. To obtain information about this book, you can write: Peterson's, P.O. Box 2123, Princeton, NJ 08543–2123. Most bookstores will be happy to order the book for you.

A number of other directories are available, although I do not recommend spending the money to buy them. Any good college or public library will have at least some of them. If you do find some of them in a library, pay attention to the publication dates. If the editions you're consulting are more than three or four years old, the information may be badly outdated. These directories include:

American Universities and Colleges, edited by American Council on Education, Washington, D.C.

Lovejoy's College Guide by Clarence E. Lovejoy, published by Simon and Schuster.

College Blue Book, published by Macmillan.

The College Handbook, published by the College Entrance Examination Board.

Comparative Guide to American Colleges by James Cass and Max Birnbaum, published by Harper and Row.

Directories like these provide brief snapshots of all (or almost all) of the accredited colleges and universities in the country, including most of the evangelical Christian colleges. You can quickly learn how many students a college has, how large its library is, how much its tuition is, whether it's accredited, what degrees it offers, and what majors you can take there.

I don't want to suggest that such directories are indispensable. Relatively few families ever consult such books. I mention them because they're available and can give you an idea of the range of colleges available within your family's geographical and financial boundaries.

Another important source of names for your list is people that you know and trust. Ask your pastor and other workers at your church for recommendations. Ask other Christian families about the colleges they and their children attended. Talk to people at work. But a warning is in order. Remember that schools can change greatly in a short period of time. Even I am amazed by the changes I have seen some colleges undergo in a few years. Keep in mind that the alumni of some colleges see their alma mater through a kind of romantic haze; the school was never really as good as they remember it, nor is it as great as they presently think it is. Schools that may have been quite average academically can improve, while schools that used to deserve their academic reputation can surrender to currents of trendy mediocrity. Colleges that were once quite conservative can turn liberal. In short, don't take the advice and opinions of other people uncritically. Remember that even pastors are not infallible in such matters. I know many who speak well of colleges that have serious problems. The pastor may be unaware of the problems or may not recognize how serious they have become.

Several Factors to Consider

In thinking about a list of possible colleges, several considerations ought to weigh heavily with the readers of this book.

Religious Considerations

It's natural to suppose that anyone reading a Christian guide to choosing a college will begin by considering several ways in which religious factors influence his or her judgment of a college. Of all the factors that might lead a Christian student or parent to include or exclude a college from his or her working list, the religious ones ought to be right up there at the top.

For example, knowledge that a particular college's religion department has a liberal bias that results in unfair attacks against important Christian beliefs and the Bible ought to count, I should think, against the college. Awareness that a different college strives to support Christian faith and practice throughout its programs ought to count as a plus. This is just one reason why I hope the working list of every family using this book will include the name of at least one evangelical Christian college. If a student is going to take courses that touch on issues important to people with Christian values (such as the Bible, Christian doctrine, and other elements of the Christian worldview), there are obvious advantages to studying in an environment that is sympathetic to and supportive of those values.[1]

Another religious consideration that many Christian families will want to consider is denominational affiliation. Many families have strong feelings about their denomination. It is not surprising then when such people find themselves pulled in the direction of a denominational college. Of course, I have already warned about cases when such families may be unaware of the extent to which a denominational college has drifted away from convictions and values they support strongly. When this is the case, the denominational college can be the worst school to choose.

For now, however, it makes sense for a Christian family to put a college on their list because it is a well-known Christian college or because it is affiliated with a denomination that they trust.

Location

Geographical location is another factor that can result in a school being added to or dropped from the list of colleges under consideration. Many families believe it's important for the student to attend a college relatively close to home. Hence, it is understandable when they give preference to a college because it is within a one day's drive of their home town. This proximity may make an occasional weekend home possible. However, it is also wise to remember that the costs of travel to and from the school are as much a college expense as tuition, books, and a dormitory room.

Careful attention should be given to the immediate environment of the college. Is it a rural campus? If so, is its distance from any large city a problem? If it's an urban school, is it in a part of the city that seems relatively safe from urban crime? Frankly, a quick glance at many urban campuses ought to be enough to lead most families to consider other options.

The issue of location raises a related matter. When it is possible, what are the advantages and disadvantages of living at home and commuting to school? The advantages are obvious: (1) College costs can be reduced considerably, or so it might appear. Room and board at residence-colleges continue to rise in cost. (2) Studying at home may prove easier than in a dormitory, where noise and interruptions can hinder concentration. (3) There are important advantages to having easy access to loved ones and familiar surroundings. Living at home does eliminate the problem of homesickness.

But living at home also has its disadvantages: (1) The financial savings may be less than you expect. Many commuting students fail to consider all of the extra expenses traveling to and from campus can involve. It's wise to figure how many miles this driving will put on a car during a year and how much this will cost in gas, tires, and repairs. (2) The length of time involved in commuting should also be considered. A ten minute drive is one thing; a two hour commute on crowded highways is another. (3) Personal interaction with other students in the kind of close environment afforded by living on campus is an important part of a total college experience. My son lived at home during his first three years in college and finally decided that he was missing too much by not staying on campus. I agreed with his judgment. (4) While dormitory life can contain its share of distractions, living at home may only subject the student to different distractions. (5) Living at home can also hinder access to such college facilities as the library and make participating in student activities more difficult.

Two things ought to count most heavily in any deliberations about commuting to college. The first is the quality of the college to which you can commute as compared with your other options. Is the college to which you can commute a school you'd attend if it were as far from home as your other top choices? The second factor that many families must consider is their ability to afford the higher costs of an education at a residence-college. If you live within commuting distance of an expensive private college, where tuition costs alone approach $20,000 a year, it's obviously much cheaper to pick a less expensive Christian college, where all costs, including room and board, are less than half this amount. On the other hand, if the school to which you can commute is a large state-supported college with a good reputation which you can attend for less than $3,000 a year, that is another matter.

Cost

Families cannot think about college for very long without the question of cost coming up. You didn't need to purchase this book to learn that college is expensive; and getting more so each year. For the 1988–89 academic year, the ten most expensive colleges in the country had average tuition costs of more than $20,000 for the year. Tuition for the most expensive college in the country, Bennington College in Vermont, was $20,590. This figure does not include fees, room and board, and costs for books, supplies, and transportation.

According to the College Board, fixed charges (that is, tuition, fees, room and board) at private, four-year colleges in the U.S. averaged $11,330 for the 1988–89 school year. When the average cost for books, supplies, and transportation is added to this figure, total costs for resident students at private, four-year colleges approached $13,000 for the year. If it's any consolation, costs at most evangelical Christian colleges were significantly lower.

For in-state students at four-year, public colleges, fixed costs averaged $4,445 for the 1988–89 school year. Out-of-state students at these same schools faced significantly higher tuition costs. Even at that, many families find it difficult to look beyond the public college or university. A savings of $5,000 a year becomes, when multiplied by four, a significant piece of change.

When considering whether your family can afford public university A or Christian college B or non-Christian college C, keep in mind that official tuition costs can be eased by various kinds of financial aid. You may not want to eliminate a college from your list because of its projected cost until you've done some study into the availability of scholarships and other financial help. Nonetheless, it would appear that only very wealthy families will give serious consideration to the more expensive colleges in the country.

The wise family will begin to face the money issue as early as possible. Parents do not do their children a favor by papering over the cost of higher education. Students need to realize how much ten or twenty thousand dollars is, how difficult it can be to pay back loans of that size, and how expensive interest costs are on such loans. At some stage early in the process, the issue of money and the options for finding that money should be discussed frankly and openly in a family roundtable.

Education in Specialized Fields
Some high school students already have an idea of the kind of vocation for which they'll be preparing in college. Naturally some vocations require specialized courses that are not available at all colleges. When this is the case, families should check to see which colleges offer training in those fields. For example, undergraduate degrees in engineering, agriculture, and some business areas are often not available at smaller four-year colleges. Many Christian liberal arts colleges do offer programs in pre-med, pre-law, education, nursing and other specialized areas. But few liberal arts colleges offer majors in more than a few such fields.

When students are reasonably sure that they are going to major in specialized fields like this, they'll want to check some of the directories mentioned earlier in this chapter to get a better idea what schools offer degrees in those areas. An important warning should be noted. Many students change their minds, especially after discovering that they have trouble getting acceptable grades in such courses. Before actually making a commitment to such a field, the student should be sure that he or she can succeed. American colleges are full of students who declared a computer science major in their freshman year but who dropped out after a semester or two. The world contains a lot of college graduates who once thought of themselves as pre-med students but who ended up majoring in history or English. The wise student considering a technical or vocational area like this will always make sure that he or she has other options, should something go wrong. The only thing worse than selecting the wrong major is continuing in that field when all signs indicate that a mistake has been made.

There is an alternative to spending all four years in a technical program at a large public university, especially if you are also interested in the advantages afforded by a Christian liberal arts college. Study carefully the general education requirements of the large university that offers the technical program you're interested in. These are the broad, general courses every college requires all of its graduates to take. They usually include one or two courses each in writing, literature, history, psychology, history, other social sciences, the natural sciences, along possibly with philosophy, religion, art, and music. With careful planning, you might want to consider spending one or two years in a Christian liberal arts college, taking general education courses identical to those stipulated in the university catalog. At the same time that you're doing this, you can take advantage perhaps of some of the Bible and theology courses offered by the Christian college. Then, after one or two years, you can transfer to the technical program that interests you.

Starting out this way has several possible benefits. It gives you the opportunity to take important liberal arts courses, where Christian values can be easily challenged, from teachers (hopefully) who share those values. Second, you may learn while doing this that the time you spend at the Christian college helps you discover new interests. For example, you may realize that you're more interested in majoring in one of the traditional liberal arts areas, like history or English, instead of a more narrow, vocationally oriented field.

Conclusion

One good way to approach the process of selecting a college is to prepare a working list of schools that you're going to look at more closely. The purpose of this chapter has been to identify some of the ways you can get names for your list.

You may get a few ideas from the list of evangelical colleges contained in the appendix of this book. Other names may be suggested by church leaders and friends. Examination of the directories mentioned earlier in this chapter may help you identify colleges that offer majors in selected fields, that fall within your family's price range, or that lie within the geographical area you prefer.

The point is to prepare a list, making sure that you have at least one good reason for placing the name of a school on that list. In later chapters, I'll discuss criteria you can use to rank these colleges, to weed some out, and to elevate one name to the top of your list.

FIVE

HOW TO REDUCE YOUR LIST OF COLLEGES

I am going to assume that you have at least made a start toward compiling a preliminary list of colleges. Take a look at it. How many schools are on the list? Next to each name, write your reason for placing the school on your list. Place a check next to the names that interest you the most. On a new piece of paper, write the names down again, but this time group them into three categories: the ones you rank highest, those you rank lowest, and the rest.

What I'm going to do in this chapter is talk about two important sources of information that can help you make further progress in ranking the colleges on your list. Once you have a preliminary idea what schools you want to look at more closely, proper use of these two sources of information is the next step in reducing your list to more manageable proportions.

The College Catalog

The easiest way to get lots of information about a college is through its catalog and other promotional material it may send with the catalog. Everyone knows this, I suppose. But what is less common is knowledge of what to look for in a catalog, knowledge of how best to use this often confusing book.

Obtaining college catalogs is easy; simply write the admissions office of the schools on your list and request one, along with the usual forms for admission, financial aid, dormitory accommodations, etc. A properly run college will have a copy of its catalog in your mailbox within a week or two. If you have to ask more than once, consider this a mark against the school. Make sure you specifically request a catalog. Catalogs have become so expensive that some colleges prefer to send other material first—usually flashy brochures full of beautiful color photos of the campus, pretty cheerleaders, and good-looking football players. But what you want at this point is not advertising but information. Get a catalog!

When the catalog arrives, write down the kinds of information I'll identify shortly. These notes should be clear enough that you can consult them later, instead of trying to find specific pages in a two or three hundred page catalog. Here are some of the more important things you should notice in a catalog.

The History and Purpose of the College

Most catalogs begin with a history of the college. This history is especially important in the case of private liberal arts colleges, many of which began as ministries of particular denominations. How old is the school? Why was it started? And, even more important, does the college still take its original mission seriously?

Catalogs then proceed to spell out what the college sees as its present mission or purpose. Pay special attention to what church-related or Christian colleges state at this point. Ask yourself if you are in sympathy with the school's objectives; if not, perhaps you'd better look elsewhere. Later, when you have the opportunity—perhaps during a visit to the school—try to determine if the present faculty and administration take the catalog's statement of the school's purpose seriously. In the case of many church-related colleges that have gone liberal, the catalogs continue to carry a statement of purpose that may be decades old but that no one connected with the college really supports anymore.

Naturally, secular colleges describe their purpose in broader, more general terms than do Christian liberal arts colleges. The catalog of my own university, for example, states that the university "provides areas of study that prepare students for careers in the arts and sciences, education, government service, business, industry, health, agriculture and similar fields. It also offers special professional and pre-professional curricula to prepare students for further professional training or for technical careers." When you think about it, this statement of purpose actually says very little. A thousand other colleges in the country claim to do the same thing.

Religious Emphases

This is not information you'll find in catalogs for public or secular colleges, but it is something you should examine very carefully in catalogs published by private colleges that claim to have a religious mission. Look to see if the college is officially related to a particular denomination. Your family should consider whether it's comfortable with this denomination. I don't know many members of Assemblies of God churches who would feel comfortable in Baptist or Presbyterian colleges. If the college is related to one of the mainline denominations, you may wish to exercise special caution. Pay careful attention to what I say about schools like this in a later chapter.

If a college purports to be a "Christian" college, it ought to contain a statement of faith, that is, a series of propositions that reports what its faculty and administration supposedly believe about God, Jesus Christ, the Holy Spirit, the Bible, salvation, and so on. Be wary of any denominational or allegedly Christian college that doesn't include a statement of faith in its catalog; the absence of one most likely indicates that the school doesn't stand for anything and doesn't expect its teachers to believe anything. Later on—perhaps during your campus visit—try to determine if the college still takes its statement of faith seriously. Many do not. I know allegedly Christian colleges that knowingly hire faculty who disagree with the statement of faith; I know allegedly Christian colleges that knowingly hire faculty who are not Christians.

Study the statement of faith. Do you and your family agree with it? Perhaps there are points you don't understand. If so, ask your pastor or someone who is likely to understand these points. Look for possible points of tension with your own understanding of Christianity. For example, so-called Holiness, or Wesleyan, schools take a position on Christian sanctification that differs from that held by many Baptists and Presbyterians. Calvinistic colleges may spell out certain positions that cause problems for families with Methodist leanings. Eschatology (the doctrine of last things) can also be a source of possible tension. In my youth, I came very close to attending a school that not only taught a different view of eschatology than the one I held, but also refused to graduate any student who disagreed with its view. I don't know if this particular school still follows that practice. But it should be clear that any school that places such emphasis on one particular interpretation of a highly complex matter may be a good place to avoid. Pay special attention to anything the statement of faith might say about the range of beliefs and practices associated with the charismatic movement. This is a very important set of issues for many people; and it is an issue that cuts both ways. Noncharismatic families may want nothing to do with a college that encourages students to speak in tongues. Strongly charismatic families may want to avoid a college that views this experience negatively.

I don't want to leave the impression that one should approach less central doctrinal differences in any rigid way.[1] It is not necessary that you be surrounded only by people who think exactly like you to have a pleasant and fruitful college experience. In fact, I happen to believe there are strong advantages (at least for certain young people) to studying in an environment where you are a bit different from the others. During my first three years of college, I found myself in strong disagreement with some of my professors. Convinced that they were wrong, I was driven to find answers to their arguments and alternatives to their positions. In order to do this, I had to read widely in books that my professors didn't even know existed. My wife and her sisters attended a Christian college that had a Wesleyan, or Holiness, orientation that was not shared by her Baptist family. They took what they wanted from this emphasis, ignored the rest, and got a good education. Given their family's financial condition and their interest in attending a Christian college relatively close to their home, it would have been foolish for them to have gone to college elsewhere.

Near the beginning of this book, I stated that the choice of a college is a very personal decision. When it comes to doctrinal disagreements among Christians, some of us can live with things that would drive others to distraction. Since the catalogs of most Christian colleges will tell you what beliefs they feel should be emphasized, study that statement of faith and ask whether you can live with it. If you can't, cross the college off your list. Then find some other school that matches your own beliefs more closely—if that is important to you.

Accreditation

The accreditation a college has is extremely important. Regrettably, some evangelical Christian colleges have failed to obtain accreditation from one of the regional accrediting associations. When a college lacks accreditation from one of these bodies, students may encounter serious difficulties if they attempt to transfer their credits elsewhere. Graduates of nonaccredited schools often have trouble getting into graduate school.

There are six regional accrediting associations in the United States. They are the New England Association of Schools and Colleges, the Middle States Association of Colleges and Secondary Schools, the Southern Association of Colleges and Schools, the North Central Association of Colleges and Schools, the Northwest Association of Colleges and Secondary Schools, and the Western Association of Schools and Colleges. Check to make sure that the college you're investigating holds accreditation from one of these bodies.

All of the better evangelical Christian colleges now have regional accreditation. However, a few Christian schools hold accreditation from a special organization that accredits only Bible colleges and schools. Some of these schools are possibly places where one can get a reasonably good education, but the lack of regional accreditation is a weakness you may want to examine more closely. Be aware that some schools that are accredited by the American Association of Bible Colleges are candidates for regional accreditation. That means that they have applied for regional accreditation and may receive it in a few years. Keep in mind, as well, that a number of evangelical schools are accredited both by the appropriate regional association and also by the American Association of Bible Colleges.

Costs

For each catalog you consult, jot down the costs of tuition, fees, and room and board. What you're after here is any significant difference in what it will cost you to attend the colleges on your list. Since the cost of books and supplies is likely to be the same at every school, you can ignore this figure for now.

Fees are an interesting device some colleges use to squeeze

extra money out of the student. I know some state-supported universities that brag that they charge no tuition for in-state students. But, when the small print is read, you learn that they do charge rather hefty registration fees. They simply take what other schools call tuition and give it a different label. Sometimes fees are a legitimate charge for students in special programs or courses. And so, a college may charge a lab fee for students taking a science course or a special music fee for music majors.

The important information here is the bottom line. Regardless of what a college calls its charges, how do the costs of college A compare with those at college B?

Financial Aid

Once you have an idea what a college charges for its services, try to learn how that cost can be reduced. A number of smaller colleges hold down costs by requiring every student to work a fixed number of hours a week. Many other schools make such work optional and pay students what is often a very nominal wage.

The colleges you're considering will have an office of financial aid. Write the head of that office for information about fellowships, scholarships, and other types of financial help. Once you learn the kinds of aid available to you along with the amount of the aid, you can get a clearer picture of the real cost of studying at that particular school. Often, you'll find, a school that appeared to be more expensive because of higher tuition turns out to be less expensive because of the availability of financial aid.

Admission Requirements

Read this section of the catalog carefully. Catalogs often stipulate that in order for a student to gain unconditional admission to the college, he or she must have taken certain high school courses, must have maintained a certain grade point average, or must have a certain ranking in the graduating class. This section of the catalog will also state whether the admissions office requires scores on the SAT or ACT exam.

Size

By size, I mean the number of students attending the college. This information is not always available from the catalog, but it is important enough to justify searching until you find it. Perhaps you can locate it in one of the college directories named in the last chapter. In the appendix to this book, I provide information about student enrollment for each of the Christian colleges mentioned.

Some colleges and universities are simply too large. My own university has 14,000 students, and I often feel that's too many. It is not uncommon for public universities to have more students than many cities have citizens. Give some thought to what it must be like to be a student on a campus that has thirty or forty thousand students—or more. If you like anonymity or being lost in a crowd, you'll love a place like that.

On the other hand, a college can also be too small. Once a school falls below a certain number of students, it's in trouble. Certainly, no school has fewer than 500 students out of choice.

Many liberal arts colleges refuse to exceed a certain size. I once taught at a Christian college that limited its student body to about 1,100 students because that was all it could seat in its chapel. As I recall, that seemed a nice size: large enough to support all of the college's programs but small enough so that everyone could know everyone else.

General Education Requirements

This is an example of catalog information that many students overlook—until they register for their first courses. Every college has certain courses that it requires all of its students to take before they can graduate. In many schools, these general education requirements will include about fifteen courses (with options) from such standard areas as composition, literature, history, natural science, social science, philosophy, religion, speech, mathematics, and the fine arts.

The general education core at some Bible colleges and smaller Christian liberal arts colleges is not always as strong as it could be. But at the other end of American higher education, a number of secular colleges have begun to water down this part of their curriculum. Under pressure from radical activists in the student body and the faculty, some colleges have begun to substitute lightweight, trendy courses for the more solid and traditional courses that used to be required. Stanford University, one of the more highly regarded universities in the country, made some regrettable moves in this direction during the 1987–88 academic year.

Students sometimes wish they could avoid some of these required courses. If the courses are taught well, they can and should be some of the most important courses you'll take in college. Approach them with a positive attitude and hope you're lucky enough to get a good teacher. In a later chapter, I'll point out one way in which many larger universities shortchange their general education students.

A rather large percentage of college freshmen enter school with no idea what areas they want to major in. This is nothing to worry about. You have at least three semesters before you have to declare a major. Wise students will use those semesters to complete their general education requirements. In many cases, students use this experience as a way of determining which fields of study interest them most. My daughter, for example, had absolutely no idea what she wanted to major in. She happened to enjoy the first courses she took in religion and sociology so much that she continued to take others. After a while, she decided to declare both sociology and religion as her majors.

Students who major in certain technical areas should be aware of a possible pitfall. Some advisers urge freshmen and sophomore majors in these areas to delay important general education courses until their junior-senior years and fill up their early years with their department's technical courses. Educationally, this is an outrageous practice. To be blunt, many of these departments are simply trying to fill their classes with warm bodies and could care less about the total educational experience of the student. Many students who have been advised in this way decide in a year or two to change their majors. But because of the bad advisement they received, they are then forced to extend their time in college by one or two years.

Areas of Study

Depending on their size and other factors, colleges and universities group their areas of study in different ways. Typically, the smallest academic unit in a college is called a department. In many cases, for example, history, government (or political science), sociology, and psychology will each be a separate department. However, there are times when colleges will lump several of these areas together, so that one finds the department of history and government. In some smaller colleges, several disciplines are joined into what is called a division. Whatever the unit is called, it will have a department head or division chair. Should you decide to major or minor in that area, that person is someone you'll get to know quite well since he or she will advise you on courses (or assign someone else as your adviser) and will sign several important forms during your college years.

In the case of a university, the academic units will be grouped into colleges. For example, a university's English department will be in the college of liberal arts, while the accounting department will be in the business college. Separate colleges within a university often have somewhat different requirements that you'll need to be aware of. For example, many business colleges require that a student have a certain grade point average during his first year or two before he can be admitted to one of the programs in the college.

Courses

College catalogs contain a list of all courses offered along with a description of those courses. If you already know what your college major will be, spend some time comparing the major requirements and courses offered by departments in different colleges. This is especially important in the case of students planning to major in religion. A properly balanced religion program will include a healthy number of courses in Bible, theology, church history, and other areas. The offerings of religion departments in most secular schools frequently slight these areas.

Faculty

Finally, it pays to look at the section of the catalog that contains information about the faculty. What does it tell you about the people who teach in your possible major? Do they have earned doctorates? Can you tell anything about the universities from which they earned their degrees?

Some weaker Christian colleges can look bad when their faculty listings are compared with those of academically stronger schools. There really isn't much excuse these days for colleges hiring faculty without earned doctorates. Of course, there are some fields where a shortage of qualified teachers with earned doctor's degrees exists: computer science, accounting, business administration, and some other areas. But this shortage does not exist in the humanities and the social sciences.

Summary

One of your most important sources of information, then, is the college catalog. Obtaining one for each school on your list will cost you only the price of a stamp. Once you get it, examine it carefully. In particular, take note of the factors I've discussed in this chapter.

Visiting the Campus

The next important source of information will cost your family some money, but it is money well-spent. There is no substitute for actually visiting a college before deciding to enroll. Some colleges require each applicant to visit the campus because they want to look you over in person. But, even if the college doesn't require a visit, you and your family should see the school for yourselves.

I recommend that you visit during a week when school is in session. If possible, try to spend a night in a dormitory—even if your parents are off campus in a motel. After all, if you attend this school, you'll have about 900 of these nights ahead of you. Eat in the dining room; you may have to eat more than 2,000 meals in the place during the next four years. Talk to students. What do they think of the college, of the faculty, of the community? What is your impression of the students? Are they pleasant? Do you like them? Are they the kind of people you want to spend four years of your life with?

If the college has a chapel service, attend it. Arrange in advance to sit in on one or two classes. I recommend that one of those classes be a religion course. Make an appointment to meet the person who will be your department head, should you enroll. Visit the financial aid office and discuss the availability of financial help.

What is your impression of the college's physical plant?

Does it look run down? What is your impression of the surrounding community? Is it safe to walk the streets after dark? Are there opportunities for part-time employment off campus? What are the dormitory rooms like? How many students are assigned to a room?

Does the school have chapters of such Christian student groups as InterVarsity, the Navigators, or Campus Crusade for Christ? Does it have the kinds of student organizations you'd like to work with?

How many campuses should you visit? That depends on how much time and money your family has to spend on this activity. It also depends on how hard you're finding it to choose among the colleges you rank highest. What is clear is this: Visiting a campus should be regarded as absolutely essential. No student should ever enroll in a college without first seeing the campus for herself.

Conclusion

I have suggested a procedure by which you and your family can acquire the names of colleges that might be of interest. I have also outlined some of the things you can do to pare that list down to one, two, or three schools. Much of the information that you'll need in making a decision is available from college catalogs. Studied carefully in the light of what you want from a college and what your family can afford, it should be possible to reduce the list of potential colleges to a small group that you and your family can visit. If my advice has been heeded, it is difficult to see why—at the conclusion of those campus visits—most families won't be able to make a reasoned decision.

Of course, there still remains a great deal more to say about all this. In the next chapter, I provide more information about the three major alternatives to studying in an evangelical Christian college. Following that, I turn my attention to the evangelical college, as I seek to explain both the strengths and weaknesses of this kind of school.

SIX

NONEVANGELICAL COLLEGES

At various points in this book, I argue that evangelical Christian families ought to look long and hard at evangelical Christian colleges that share and support their values. Colleges like this receive a rather lengthy analysis in chapters seven and eight. Since it is not always possible for young people from Christian families to attend an evangelical college, it makes sense in a book like this to say something about the other options. In this chapter, I will say a bit about three kinds of other schools: the public university, the secular private college, and the nonevangelical denominational college.

The Public University

Most of the public colleges and universities I'll discuss in this section are state-supported universities. For the record, I probably should note that some public universities are supported largely by funds provided by cities. The City University of New York, the University of Cincinnati, and the University of Louisville are three schools that, at least, started out in this way. Many municipal colleges and universities now receive some percentage of their budget from the state government.

In many states, there is a rather clear-cut distinction, in terms of financial support and prestige, between the major state university and so-called regional universities. In the state of Illinois, for example, the University of Illinois at Champaign/Urbana gets most of the attention in the state. Illinois' regional universities have such names as Northern Illinois and Southern Illinois. This tendency to identify regional universities exists in many other states such as Kentucky (Western Kentucky University and Eastern Kentucky University), Colorado (Northern Colorado), and Florida (the University of South Florida and the University of West Florida).

Outside the northeast, residents of some states get carried away by their enthusiasm for the football and basketball teams of the major university in the state. This often results in a rather common kind of irrational behavior in which thousands of high school graduates choose a university primarily because of its athletic teams. These young people know nothing about the academic reputation of these schools. All they know is that they love "the Big Blue" (Kentucky), "the Big Orange" (Tennessee), or "the Big Red" (Indiana). I cannot imagine a worse way to select a college.

Several states also have large, state-supported technical schools. Examples include Texas Tech, Texas A. and M., Georgia Tech, and Virginia Tech. Many southern states also have public colleges that used to be exclusively for black students. While schools like Kentucky State and Tennessee State have taken major strides toward integration, they continue to be primarily black institutions.

State universities are often very big places. Ohio State University in Columbus has about 53,000 students! Ohio's regional universities are big enough in their own right. Bowling Green State University has about 17,000, while Kent State has approximately 20,000 students. The University of Michigan's student enrollment comes in at around 35,000, while Michigan

State's tops 42,000. Indiana University has around 33,000 students, while to the north of Bloomington, Purdue University has one or two thousand less.

Schools this size are obviously big enough to offer courses and programs in just about any area that any person might want to study. While no one, either in the administration of these schools or in the state legislatures that provide the tax dollars, ever asks whether all these programs can be justified on academic grounds, the public monies keep pouring in, and the students keep pouring out.

Because of the support they receive from tax dollars, public universities have an enormous and often unfair advantage over private colleges. The public universities are much cheaper to attend. Because private colleges, which often offer a superior education, are forced to charge much higher tuition, they find it increasingly difficult to compete in the race to recruit students.

But there is no question about it: The public university offers considerable financial savings over most private colleges. Because of its size, it also can offer a much greater diversity of programs and courses. It is often a tempting choice for families on a tight budget.

Most of the Christian families I know who have settled on a public university as their first choice cite one or two reasons for their choice. The first is money. The significantly lower cost of attending a public university over against a much more expensive private college often tips the scales. A separate but related reason occurs in cases when the public college or university is also within commuting distance of the family's home. The family then gets the benefits of both eliminating the expense of room and board and lowering tuition costs.

The other reason that is hard to argue against arises in situations where the student knows (or believes) that he or she is going to specialize in some professional or preprofessional area that may not be offered by the Christian colleges that might otherwise interest him or her. There may also be good reason to believe that even if the program is available in a Christian college, the one offered in the larger and better financed state university is superior. This is often true, for example, in areas like computer science. I have already warned, however, against making too much of this matter. The world often looks quite different to students by the time they reach their second or third year in college. They may discover new interests, or their grades may fall below acceptable limits. It is wise to be flexible and leave yourself other options if things don't work out as you planned. There is merit in a suggestion I made earlier in the book: Consider taking your first year or two of general education courses in a fully accredited, Christian liberal arts college and then transfer those credits to the public university where you'll pursue your technical or specialized program.

If there are some good reasons for selecting a public college, there are also some negatives that ought to be considered carefully. For one thing, the sheer size of many of these schools ought to make them unappealing to many people. Nothing can bring this home more quickly than a personal visit to one of these small cities. Spend some time walking around the huge campus while the college is in session and ask yourself whether you really want to submerge yourself in this anonymous mass of humanity.

Because these schools are so large, it is impossible to get to know more than a small percentage of the faculty and students. That is a high price to pay. Talk to people who graduated from smaller colleges where they were part of a community. As one book puts it, "the ultimate value of a college education derives not simply from taking classes or passing exams but from the ongoing, loving, painful, growth-inducing human interactions that take place on campus at all hours of the day and night, throughout the academic year."[1] The quality of this important process at huge public universities cannot compare with that afforded by many smaller colleges.

At such large colleges (and this is equally true of many large private universities), students often have little voice in choosing their instructors. Since there may be 50 or 100 or more sections of a required course in English or history or psychology, you simply get in a line and take whatever teacher you're given. Because there are so many teachers, you will probably have no idea how good or bad this professor is until it is too late to drop the course without penalty. Even worse, there will be many times when the teacher you end up with is a graduate student who may be teaching his first class. You may have selected this large university because of what you believed about the quality of its professors. The irony is that many of the courses you take during your first two years may end up being taught by students who are still years away from completing their doctor's degree. I will have more to say about this graduate student situation and a related problem that exists at many large private universities later in this chapter.

I will mention just one additional problem often encountered at public colleges: Student advisement is often handled by people who don't know or don't really care about what they're doing. On some campuses, student advisement is turned over to graduate students in the college of education. In most cases, these students' education in the arts and sciences is deficient. Because many of these student advisers don't know much about philosophy or history or physics or computer science, any advice they purport to give is tainted by their own lack of experience and knowledge. Of course, I could relate many horror stories about the poor advisement even the faculty can give on such campuses. I have already mentioned how often I have encountered students who began their college programs as majors in very narrow, technical areas. Their departmental advisers continually pushed them into a narrow band of courses related to that major during their first two years in college, thus forcing the students to delay their more basic college work in general education courses until late in their programs. In many cases (and this was usually when I saw them), the students discovered after two years that they were no longer interested in the technical program. Because of the terrible advice received from faculty in that program, most of their course work during those years was a total loss. When this happens, what should be a four-year degree stretches out to five and six years, with a corresponding increase in financial cost.

The contrast between all this and the situation at many smaller colleges should be obvious. Think about being a student on a campus where you know every teacher and student, and they know you. Imagine a situation where each of your teachers is selected by you and not by a computer. Think what it must be like to be on a campus where every course is taught by a regular faculty member and not by some graduate student. Reflect also about the advantages of a place where your adviser is a faculty member, who not only knows you as an individual but who even cares about you and your future.

Nothing I've said in this section is meant to suggest that one cannot be happy or get a good education at a large public university. Nor is it the case that the problems I've mentioned are this bad at every state university. But these negatives ought to be considered by the families reading this book. You have every right to expect that you'll get what you pay for.

Secular Private Colleges

A private college, of course, is one that is not supported by taxpayers' money. Private colleges and universities may be divided into religious schools (those that have a publicly acknowledged religious mission or some tie to a Christian denomination) and those that are secular, that is, have no such mission or tie.[2] It is this latter group of schools that I'll discuss in this section of the chapter.

Colleges in this category vary greatly in size. Smaller schools of this type may have only several hundred students, while the biggest of them rival public universities in size. To mention just one example, Syracuse University has well over 20,000 students.

These schools also differ greatly in the quality of their academic programs. It should be noted, however, that when many people in the U.S. are asked to identify the best colleges and universities in the country, the schools most often mentioned are private universities. Such lists often include schools like Harvard, Yale, Stanford, Duke, and Vanderbilt. Many of the best-known, private secular colleges in the nation were started by Christian denominations. This was true, for example, of Princeton University, Brown University, and the University of Chicago, as well as Harvard, Yale, Duke, and Vanderbilt. Over the years, that religious or denominational tie first weakened and then was cut. To say that a private college is secular means that it is independent of any church, ecclesiastical, or denominational control.

Many private secular colleges are strictly four-year institutions. But, as the names of the schools mentioned in the last paragraph indicate, many others include graduate schools that offer some of the most highly respected doctor's degrees in the country. In fact, the reputation that many of these schools have is perhaps the major reason why families that can afford it make them their college of choice. Of course, the best of these colleges are also very difficult to get into. And so they cost more and have higher entrance requirements than most public universities.

What are the major drawbacks to colleges like this? To begin with, it is helpful to remember that some private colleges offer an inferior education. Being private is not synonymous with excellence. It pays to examine carefully the quality of education provided by any private secular schools on your list. Second, you need to realize that one can encounter significant hostility to evangelical Christianity on such campuses. Naturally, this can also be a problem in state universities; it can be even a greater problem in theologically liberal denominational colleges. But it is something that wise and prepared families will anticipate.

Those private universities that offer doctoral degrees often engage in one or two practices that can have a significantly negative effect on the quality of undergraduate education. The problem arises in connection with how the university chooses to cover its freshman and sophomore general education courses, which often involve hundreds of students. In many cases, these required courses are simply turned over to graduate students—something never mentioned in the university catalog. This results in a situation where a family selects a very expensive college because of the reputation of the school's regular faculty. What the family doesn't realize is that many of the first courses their child takes at that expensive school will not be taught by regular faculty members; they will be taught instead by students who may still be several years away from their doctorate. In fact, many of these student teachers will never complete their doctoral program.

Larger private universities (and this also holds true for many public universities as well) sometimes handle the problem of beginning level courses in a different way. In this second case, the university simply piles 500 to 1,000 students into a large lecture hall where they hear lectures once or twice a week by regular members of the faculty. In all fairness, some of these professors have become rather good at presenting entertaining and informative presentations to such large audiences. Of course, some also do a bad job. Once every week or so, the large body of students is then divided into smaller discussion sections where the ever-present graduate student leads a discussion of points made in the professor's lecture and the textbook. I will leave it to the reader to decide whether the graduate student or the professor reads the term papers and grades the examinations for courses like this. Even when the regular professor does glance over the exams after the graduate student has graded them, the impersonal nature of the setting results in a much less desirable educational experience than can often be had in a smaller college where classes, limited in size, are taught exclusively by regular faculty members.

If I were a parent about to spend a great deal of money to send my child to a large and prestigious university, thinking that she would be taught by some of the top educators in the country, I'd be a little unhappy to discover how little contact she was actually going to have with these professors.

My point is that just because a school is an expensive private college is no reason to assume that the quality of education there is necessarily better than what might be found elsewhere. Perhaps the family will ask different questions about the private college than of the public university. But both kinds of colleges should receive the same careful scrutiny.

Nonevangelical Denominational Colleges

Private religious colleges that make some claim to being Protestant can be divided into those that are evangelical (a term I explain in the next paragraph) and those that are not. I must admit there are times when no sharp line can be found—when it is difficult to say precisely where a college lies on the theological spectrum. Most Protestant colleges were evangelical at one time. As many of them became increasingly liberal in their understanding of the Bible and Christian beliefs, there were times when the wheat and the tares on their campuses were growing side by side. Even after the tares took over, the administration of the colleges continued to claim an evangelical commitment that no longer existed in order to receive continued financial support from uninformed members of the denomination.

The word *evangelical* is the contemporary word that refers to Protestants who fit the following description. First, evangelicals are theologically orthodox in the sense that they accept the teachings of the early Christian creeds. Evangelicals believe in the Trinity, the deity of Christ, the Incarnation, the substitutionary Atonement, the bodily resurrection of Christ, justification by faith, and other essential elements of historic Christianity. Evangelicals take the Bible to be their ultimate authority in matters of faith and practice. Evangelicals have had a religious experience that is sometimes described by such words as *conversion* and *born again*. And evangelicals are interested in leading others to the same kind of conversion experience.

There is nothing new about this list of convictions. In fact, until after the Civil War, every mainline Church in America—the Methodist, Presbyterian, Baptist, Lutheran, and Episcopalian—was evangelical in its theology.[3] Slowly at first, the evangelical consensus in America's mainline denominations began to crumble under the assault of liberal views from Europe that gradually took root in the seminaries of the mainline denominations. The attacks were directed first toward the integrity and authority of Scripture. After that important ground had been captured, the growing liberal presence in the mainline denominations began to question such essential Christian beliefs as the deity of Christ and the bodily resurrection.

Protestant liberalism was a religion without a personal God, without a divine Savior, without an inspired Bible, and without a life-transforming conversion. It was, in fact, a totally new religion that insisted on retaining the Christian label. By the end of the 1920s, this new religion had gained control of denominational schools, publications, mission boards, and, eventually, total control of the mainline denominations.

The colleges I have in view in this section of the chapter are officially related in some way to the predominantly liberal mainline denominations. For example, the United Methodist Church has eighty-one colleges and eight universities. The Presbyterian Church (U.S.A.), a recent merger of the northern and southern branches of Presbyterianism, claims some seventy-one related colleges. The Evangelical Lutheran Church, a recent merger of the American Lutheran Church and the Lutheran Church in America, claims a relationship to some forty-four colleges and seminaries. The Christian Church (Disciples) maintains a tie to thirty-six colleges, seminaries, and undergraduate schools of religion. There are twenty-seven colleges and universities in fellowship with the American Baptist Church. The United Church of Christ can identify more than fifty colleges with which it has some kind of relationship. The number of Episcopalian colleges and universities is ten.

With only a few exceptions, these denominational colleges regard themselves as enemies of evangelical Christianity.[4] They are theologically liberal. They often are also ardent defenders of any liberal cause that happens to be trendy at the moment. In the current climate of America, this puts many of them on the side of Marxism, anti-Americanism, homosexuality, abortion, and radical feminism.

In fact, if it were not for the fact that these schools still retain some kind of tie to a Christian denomination, it would be difficult to find any justification for regarding them as Christian colleges. Many faculty members at these schools see the undermining of evangelical Christianity as a major task for themselves and their colleges. As James Davison Hunter points out, "Christian higher education historically evolved into precisely the opposite of what it was supposed to be, that is, into bastions of secularity if not anti-Christian sentiment."[5]

Many of these liberal, church-related colleges played an important role in the movement of their denominations away from the historic Christian faith. Colleges that had been established to defend the faith became the tool by which that faith was undermined and largely removed from the mainline churches. Because of their past use as instruments of change, many of the people associated with these schools continue to see themselves in this role. Pity the innocent, uninformed, and unprepared evangelical student who wanders into the path of these people. Educating such a young person, for these professors, is synonymous with getting him to reject his evangelical faith.

It is for this reason that I find it difficult—whenever there is a choice—to recommend one of these theologically liberal schools. Many of them are far more hostile to biblical Christianity than secular colleges. And because students often enter such "Christian" colleges with their guard down, it is much easier for such schools to negatively affect the religious beliefs of the evangelical student than for supposedly more secular environments where more students have their guard up.

For many young people, the worst place to go to college is a school where they believe the professors can be trusted theologically and spiritually. The student puts down her guard and, before she knows it, she is accepting uncritically all kinds of claims that she might have challenged on a secular campus. Regrettably, this sort of thing is occurring with increasing regularity on the campuses of church-related colleges that are related to more conservative denominations.

Conclusion

The largest number of evangelical young people by far choose to attend college at one of the types of schools discussed in this chapter. Their evaluations of their colleges—along with the effect those schools may have had on their Christian beliefs—are as varied as the colleges they attended. None of us should be surprised to hear that the same college has had a vastly different effect on different students. The important point for evangelical families to remember is the urgency of getting the most complete picture possible of the issues identified in this chapter.

SEVEN

EVANGELICAL CHRISTIAN COLLEGES

The evangelical Christian college differs from the liberal denominational colleges described at the end of the last chapter in several ways. First, the evangelical college makes no apology for its commitment to Jesus Christ, to the inspired and authoritative Word of God, and to the essential doctrinal beliefs that have defined the nature of historic Christianity. This is evident in the doctrinal statement that most of these colleges place prominently in their catalogs. The evangelical college is not simply Christian in name. It is self-consciously Christian. Therefore, it works hard to see that every member of its administration and faculty is a committed Christian believer. Moreover, it checks continually to see that its faculty accept unreservedly its doctrinal statement. The good evangelical college sees no inconsistency between its Christian mission and its role as an academic institution. In all honesty, I have found a greater commitment to academic excellence at many of the evangelical colleges I am familiar with than at many secular schools that have (undeservedly) somewhat better reputations.

In spite of the fact that evangelical colleges offer Christian families more for their educational dollar than any other kind of school, the total enrollment at all of these colleges combined is less than 90,000. This is fewer students than you could find at two large state universities.

Some Differences

Christian families will quite naturally look for different things in the colleges they consider. Some of these schools belong to theologically conservative denominations, a fact that makes them attractive to families in the same denomination. But many Christian families are interested in a particular theological emphasis that may transcend more narrow denominational boundaries. For example, many such families regard the doctrine of biblical inerrancy as so important that they would avoid a college from their own denomination that ignored or denied the doctrine—if they were aware of the fact. Some evangelicals are fundamentalists or pentecostals and want to see those convictions emphasized in whatever college they select. Other evangelicals think it's important to avoid fundamentalist or pentecostal schools and select colleges more representative of mainstream evangelicalism. Because some people may have difficulty defining these terms, a brief explanation may help. The words *mainstream evangelicalism, fundamentalism,* and *pentecostalism* certainly point to three ways in which evangelical colleges can differ.

Fundamentalism, Pentecostalism, and the Evangelical Mainstream

I have already explained that the word *evangelical* is the contemporary term used to refer to theologically conservative Protestants in America. One can normally expect that anyone who claims to be an evangelical is a Christian believer whose theology is traditional, or orthodox, who takes the Bible as his or her ultimate authority in matters of faith and practice, who has had a religious conversion (is born again), and who is interested in leading others to the same kind of conversion experience.

There are three major branches of evangelicalism, a fact that can be illustrated by three intersecting circles. The center circle represents what some have called the *evangelical mainstream*. What this means is that evangelicals who are neither fundamentalists nor pentecostals can be said to belong to the very large and rather ill-defined center of the evangelical movement. The evangelical mainstream is typified by leaders like Billy Graham, publications like *Christianity Today*, and colleges like Wheaton College.

One of the circles that intersects that evangelical mainstream represents *fundamentalism*. The fact that the fundamentalist circle is not coextensive with the evangelical mainstream illustrates that some fundamentalists do not wish to be identified with evangelicalism. One difference between a fundamentalist and a mainstream evangelical lies in their different attitudes. Fundamentalists tend to be a bit more combative about their convictions. They also tend to emphasize a greater number of beliefs and practices as tests of orthodoxy. For example, a mainstream evangelical will often stress the importance of believing in Christ's Second Coming, and let it go at that. A fundamentalist will frequently think there's something seriously wrong with you if you deviate in any way from his detailed, pretribulational, premillennial eschatology.[1] More extreme fundamentalists are also characterized by the practice of separatism; they insist that true fundamentalists keep themselves apart from worldly people, from liberals, and from mainstream evangelicals, whom they often accuse of compromise.

The situation gets even more complicated when you realize that there are different kinds of fundamentalists. Fundamentalist leaders like Jerry Falwell are actually moderate fundamentalists. While Falwell is quite proud of the fundamentalist label, he is basically just a very conservative evangelical. Moderate fundamentalism is represented by people like Falwell, by publications like *The Fundamentalist Journal,* and by colleges like Liberty University. The more extreme type of fundamentalist is represented by people like Bob Jones, by colleges like Bob Jones University and Tennessee Temple University, and by denominations like the General Assembly of Regular Baptists (G.A.R.B.).

The third intersecting circle is *pentecostalism,* that branch of Christianity that emphasizes the continuing relevance and importance of such charismatic gifts as speaking in tongues and physical healing. Pentecostalism itself is divided into many factions and, of course, some of its more prominent figures, such as Jim Bakker and Jimmy Swaggart, have not represented either pentecostalism, evangelicalism, or Christianity very well these past few years. Perhaps the most well-known pentecostal figures, other than Swaggart, are Oral Roberts and Pat Robertson of the CBN television network and its show, *The 700 Club.* The largest pentecostal denomination is the Assemblies of God. Of course, the pentecostal or charismatic movement has also made significant inroads into many denominations, including the Episcopal Church and the United Methodist Church. Pat Robertson is himself a Southern Baptist.

Denominational Differences

Evangelical colleges can also be distinguished denominationally. Many of these schools are nondenominational or interdenominational which simply means that they have no official ties to any specific denomination. Gordon College, Asbury College, Wheaton College, and Westmont College are four examples of interdenominational schools.

Other evangelical colleges are related to various conservative or evangelical denominations. The following list (which is not intended to be complete) names a number of these denominations along with one or two of that church body's colleges:

Assemblies of God—Evangel College plus several Bible colleges

Baptist General Conference—Bethel College (St. Paul, Minnesota)

Baptist (independent)—Liberty University, Tennessee Temple University

Christian and Missionary Alliance—Nyack College, Toccoa Falls College

Christian Reformed Church—Calvin College

Church of God (Anderson, Indiana)—Anderson College

Church of God (Cleveland, Tennessee)—Lee College

Church of the Nazarene—several colleges including Southern Nazarene University

Churches of Christ—many schools including David Lipscomb University

Evangelical Free Church—Trinity College

Free Methodist—Roberts Wesleyan College, Seattle Pacific University, and others

Free Will Baptist—Free Will Baptist Bible College

General Association of Regular Baptists—several including Cedarville College

Presbyterian Church in America—Covenant College

Reformed Church in America—Northwestern College (Iowa)

Wesleyan Church—Houghton College and Indiana Wesleyan University

A number of evangelical colleges, plus some others that could be viewed as borderline cases, are affiliated with mainline denominations. For example, Grove City College and King College (Tennessee) are strong evangelical schools that are affiliated with the Presbyterian Church (U.S.A.). It is sometimes more difficult to sort things out with some other mainline colleges. Both Eastern College and Judson College are affiliated with the American Baptist Church and view themselves as evangelical. Some other American Baptist colleges have made their break with evangelicalism indisputably clear.

Some Other Theological Differences

My earlier discussion of fundamentalism and pentecostalism certainly touches on some of the ways in which evangelicals differ theologically. Our denominational differences also reflect theological disagreements. But evangelicals and their colleges divide along other theological fault-lines as well. One of the most widely encountered of these is the set of disagreements that divides us into Calvinists and Arminians.[2] Colleges that represent the Calvinist, or Reformed, position include Calvin College, Dordt College, Northwestern College in Iowa, and Trinity Christian College near Chicago. The Arminian perspective is represented by such nondenominational schools as Asbury College, as well as by colleges affiliated with such denominations as the Free Methodist Church, the Wesleyan Church, the Church of the Nazarene, and the Assemblies of God.

A related area of disagreement concerns the doctrine of sanctification. The Reformed view of sanctification, which stresses personal growth in holiness that always, in this life, falls short of complete sanctification, can be found at colleges that stress Calvinism. A different understanding of this doctrine is found among Christians who take a Wesleyan, or Holiness, approach. This second view is never found among non-Arminians. Consequently, students attending a Free Methodist college like Roberts Wesleyan or a Wesleyan school like Houghton or a Nazarene college will find much more emphasis placed upon a Christian experience subsequent to conversion that introduces the believer into a quality of Christian living often described with words like *the deeper life*. Of course, the postconversion experience that pentecostals seek under the name, *baptism in the Holy Spirit*, is supposed to be accompanied by the outward sign of speaking in tongues. Any Christian who takes any of these competing positions seriously is likely to feel out of place at a college that disagrees.

I will mention just one more area of potential disagreement: dispensationalism.[3] This view, commonly associated with the Scofield Reference Bible, is a staple of fundamentalist Baptists. But it is widely held among many pentecostal groups, including the Assemblies of God. It is strongly opposed by many Presbyterians and other Reformed Christians. Among the colleges that insist on a dispensational approach to the Bible are such schools as Grace College, Grand Rapids Baptist College, Biola University, Baptist Bible College, Liberty University, and Bryan College.

Some Strengths

There is, of course, no such thing as the perfect college. Nor is there any such thing as the perfect evangelical college. Each has its drawbacks. But it would be hard to have missed the fact that I believe there are some important advantages to studying at a solid evangelical school.

For one thing, a number of these colleges are excellent academic institutions. For many years, Calvin College in Grand Rapids, Michigan, has had one of the most highly regarded philosophy departments in the country. Of course (and perhaps unfortunately) few high school graduates are interested in studying much philosophy. And, equally worth noting, a college that may have a few outstanding departments may have other features that make it unattractive. Many evangelicals will disapprove of Calvin's generally liberal stance on political issues or its loose attitude toward many issues of Christian liberty. As always, each family has to make up its own mind on what issues it thinks are important. When you correspond with the colleges on your list, ask each one if it can provide information about its academic reputation.

Second, the evangelical college's support for the beliefs and values of the Christian family is another positive consideration. There is a great deal to be said for attending a school where these beliefs are supported, instead of being torn down or ridiculed.

Third, the Christian College Coalition is correct when it states that, "What sets Christian colleges apart from other institutions—more than size or academic offerings or denominational ties—is the educational environment: the culture of living and learning, sharing and caring."[4] One of the most important and frequently overlooked aspects of a college education is the role that being part of a small, learning and caring community for four years plays in the development of the student.

On other kinds of campuses, learning and faith are divorced from each other. If the Christian student wants to integrate his personal faith with what he's learning in the classroom, he has to do it himself. But, "at Christian liberal arts colleges," the Christian College Coalition correctly notes, "the integration of faith and learning is an ongoing quest."[5] When Christian professors on Christian campuses are doing their job properly (and sometimes they don't), the student will be helped to see how Christian beliefs and the Bible relate to what is being learned in history, literature, the natural sciences, and the social sciences.

Finally, the best Christian colleges offer their students something they cannot find in private colleges and state-supported universities that may have more money to play around with. The evangelical college can offer an approach to education that helps the student become a whole person, that enables the student to tie all the important aspects of her intellectual, moral, spiritual, and religious life together. I agree with the statement that "a college education should be much more than simply a stepping stone for getting a job. Rather, it should provide a solid foundation for living an active, meaningful, concerned, contributing life in God's world."[6] A good college should be concerned with much more than what its students learn; it should also be concerned with the kind of men and women those students become. The ancient Greeks recognized that excellence (virtue) is not intellectual alone. The good human being is the well-rounded individual: sound of mind, strong in body, and healthy in spirit. A good college should be concerned with educating the whole human being, and this includes saying something about moral and spiritual values.

Some Weaknesses

It is clear then that the right student studying at the right evangelical college can get things that no public or private, secular or liberal denominational college can begin to provide. Unfortunately, I must now admit that evangelical colleges also have some problems, some of them serious.

Some of these schools are long on spirituality but short on academics. The people running the show at some of the weaker evangelical colleges have yet to see that Christianity has nothing to fear from any area of human knowledge. Some of these colleges have dragged their feet in upgrading their faculty. There are thousands of unemployed Ph.D.'s representing many academic fields; some of them are evangelicals. And yet, some evangelical colleges still have many faculty members without earned doctorates. That is a situation that is impossible to justify. I have already stated that some of the strongest colleges in the nation are evangelical colleges; I must now admit that some of the weakest schools are as well. Hence, it is important that you look carefully at the academic strength of the schools on your list.

It is also true that some evangelical schools evidence a noticeable wobbling on important theological matters. I know for a fact that some of these schools don't take their doctrinal statements seriously any more. I also know a number of colleges still want the public to think they're theologically sound, when, in fact, they are rapidly moving away from the evangelical camp.

Evangelical colleges play a special role within the evangelical community. Degrees from certain schools tend to certify the holder of the degree as religiously "safe," as someone that evangelical churches can trust. Moreover, many Christian parents see such colleges as safe places for their children to be educated. Unfortunately, we have reached a stage in the history of the church where both families and the evangelical community at large should consider whether a review of this whole matter is in order. I have talked to many bitter and disillusioned parents who sent their children to this or that evangelical college, believing that it was as "safe" as when they went there twenty years ago. To their grief, these parents learned how quickly a college can change. In the cases I am thinking about, the children now have a weaker faith or no faith at all. Often they have been turned into left-wing radicals by evangelical professors who can't tell the difference between the message of an Old Testament prophet like Amos and the message of a social radical like Karl Marx.

The growth of liberal tendencies at a number of evangelical colleges was discussed more than ten years ago by author Richard Quebedeaux in a book titled *The Worldly Evangelicals*. He began by drawing attention to the influence of liberalism in schools associated with the Southern Baptist Convention.[7] His claim has been supported by noted evangelical theologian, Carl F. H. Henry, who wrote that the Southern Baptist Convention "in several of its seminaries espouses a murky neoorthodoxy; [and] some of its colleges, no longer unapologetically Christian, even hire faculty members who make no profession of faith whatever."[8]

Quebedeaux noted that Oral Roberts University has avoided any statement of faith that might reveal where its faculty is supposed to stand theologically. Given the lack of any theological foundation at Oral Roberts, Quebedeaux was not surprised to find the theological faculty at the school drifting in the direction of existentialism and theological liberalism.[9]

According to Quebedeaux, the governing boards of several evangelical colleges are aware of liberal tendencies at the schools. "They know that many of their faculty sign the required statement of faith tongue in cheek. The same attitude pertains to faculty and students who break the conduct code (or pledge) imposed by some colleges banning gambling, alcohol, tobacco, pot and social dancing on and off campus."[10] Quebedeaux continued by saying:

> What *does* concern the governing boards of these colleges, however, is that the infringement of doctrinal standards and rules of conduct remain a local, "in house" matter. As long as professors do not publish their liberal views in widely circulated popular magazines read by conservative financial backers of these institutions, much can be tolerated.[11]

Quebedeaux shocked a lot of people by including some of the best-known and most highly respected evangelical colleges in his discussion. For example, he wrote that some of the faculty at Wheaton College are "moving farther to the left, both in [their] utilization of critical methods and in the cultural attitudes and politics of its faculty."[12]

Quebedeaux also referred to those evangelicals

> who may still *believe* like evangelicals, but wish to *behave* like liberals. Furthermore, among this group there may be an increasingly large number of people who really *have* moved beyond evangelical belief toward liberalism. In other words,

they have rejected the evangelical position intellectually (though they may not admit or even recognize it), but they still have an *emotional* attachment to the movement in which they were converted and nurtured.[13]

Quebedeaux's damning comments were met by stony silence from the evangelical colleges he commented on. History shows that once Christian colleges begin to drift, only occasionally, and then only under strong and assertive leadership, do they ever recover.

Once in a while, the tensions at this or that evangelical college will rise to the surface in the form of some publication that draws public attention to the matter. Something like this happened during the summer of 1985 when Edward Ericson, Jr., an English professor at Calvin College, no longer found it possible to keep silent about some things occurring on his campus. His remarks appeared as an editorial in the August, 1985, issue of *The Reformed Journal*.[14]

Ericson began by noting how, in the secular world, the tide of political radicalism had largely receded. However, as the old radicalism has retreated in the secular world, it has surfaced on the campuses of evangelical colleges and seminaries, including his own school, Calvin College. He found it bizarre that years after radicalism had ceased to be chic in the secular world, evangelicals mouth its platitudes "as if it were a new and viable intellectual alternative." For these new evangelical radicals, three major tenets are paramount: "the self-aggrandizing romance with corrupt Third Worldism . . . the casual indulgence of Soviet totalitarianism. . . . [and] the hypocritical and self-dramatizing anti-Americanism which is the New Left's bequest to mainstream politics." Evangelical radicals, Ericson observed, have little or nothing to say about what communism has done to Ethiopia, Afghanistan, or Nicaragua.

Ericson also expressed his concern about the extent to

which the traditional curriculum of Christian colleges is being radicalized by some professors. Courses that allow radical professors to promote Marxist ideology raise questions of one sort. But for a growing number of radicalized professors, the end or goal of education is not knowledge or truth but what Marxists call *praxis*. What bothered Ericson was the hidden agenda of those who talk about "internationalizing" the curriculum of evangelical colleges. He wrote:

> I see no indication that those who want to internationalize the curriculum are panting for our students to know that 66,000,000 human beings died in the [Soviet Union's] Gulag Archipelago or that Communists killed a third of all Cambodians in just a few years [a number estimated at two and a half million]. . . . No, I think that they will want to tell our students that the United States is an aggressor state which patronizes such unbearable client states as South Africa and Israel, and they will want us to leave the Communist rulers of the Nicaraguans to their own devices. And all of this agenda they will justify by observing that Christ was on the side of the poor and the oppressed (*their* chosen poor and oppressed). There is a special moral urgency, they will say, to the causes which they espouse. The justifications offered will be always spiritual ones, never political ones.

Ericson is but one of many evangelicals who regard this kind of radicalism as a serious threat to evangelicalism in general and to the evangelical college in particular.[15]

A few years ago, I spent several days participating in a rather small conference with a group of people who teach sociology at various evangelical colleges. After just a few hours (long enough for everyone around the table to speak), I realized that almost every sociologist at that table was a Marxist of one type or another.[16] Their professional training had so indoctrinated them that they brought Marxist assumptions and categories of thinking with them to their teaching of sociology. But, while their teaching of sociology at evangelical colleges was controlled by Marxist presuppositions, I saw absolutely no signs that these Christian sociologists were even aware of the powerful philosophical and economic arguments against the views they accepted so uncritically.

In 1987, Douglas W. Frank, who was then teaching at a branch of Trinity College, published a book titled *Less Than Conquerors: How Evangelicals Entered the Twentieth Century*.[17] The appearance of his book prompted Richard John Neuhaus, a respected Lutheran theologian, to comment on how various statements made in Frank's book can better help us see just where the evangelical radicals are heading. "As surely as Pat Robertson advances a 'biblical politics' of the right," Neuhaus observes, "Douglas Frank and others advance a biblical politics of the left. A significant difference is that Robertson admits to what he is doing, while those on the left adamantly assert that they are above and beyond politics. Curiously, they are often to be heard asserting this while simultaneously agitating for their own quite specific political agenda."[18]

> Frank's embrace of a Marxian class analysis of America's consumerist, imperialist, capitalist sins is of only modest interest in this connection. Here he is but repeating a received wisdom, which in his case gives every appearance of being quite newly received. More interesting is his polemic against national security, armaments, and so forth. This is more interesting because it is theologically related to his understanding of the powerlessness to which Christians are called. . . . Frank would undoubtedly insist that he is not anti-American, since the strictures against the principalities and powers apply equally to, say, the Soviet Union. But, of course, criticism should begin at home, and therefore it is against our American aspirations to security, power and influence that we must set ourselves if we are to exemplify the radical powerlessness of the Gospel. And, of course, those who subscribe to that view make no secret of the fact that

they wish they had the power to implement their program of powerlessness. It does get a trifle convoluted.[19]

I will mention just one more book in connection with this discussion of the fact that a troubling weakness at a growing number of evangelical colleges is an uncritical surrender to the political ideology of the radical left. The book is *The Survival of the Adversary Culture* by Paul Hollander.[20]

Many people think that little survives from the radical critiques and rejection of American society that we remember so well from the 1960s and 1970s. Paul Hollander disagrees. It is true, he admits, that many of the older radical movements and organizations seemed to have disappeared for several years. But, while they were publicly less visible, they continued to survive and grow below the surface. By the late 1980s, the adversary culture had resurfaced with a vengeance. While in its earlier incarnations the adversary culture was part of the counterculture, many of its beliefs, values, and attitudes have become part of mainstream America. During the 1968 Democratic convention, the representatives of the adversary culture were outside the convention rioting in the streets. During the 1988 Democratic convention, they were inside helping to run the show.

Without question, Hollander points out, the place where this radicalism is most evident is the college campus, where large numbers of the faculty go about the task of politicizing their disciplines and their campuses. The campus is one place where the dispositions of the old adversary culture (the mindset of the radicals of the 1960s and 1970s) still thrive. The survival of the adversary culture is also apparent in the statements and actions of the liberals who compose the hierarchies of America's so-called mainline denominations. Surprisingly, its influence continues to grow in many pockets of American evangelicalism, especially on the campuses of respected evangelical colleges and seminaries. Parents who want an accurate picture of how radicalized college professors, including many on evangelical campuses, are thinking these days—if *thinking* is not too strong a word—should consider reading Hollander's book.

I must take the time to consider a possible objection or two from representatives of the evangelical colleges I've been criticizing. Some will reply that when a good college does its job properly, students will frequently take what they've learned and head in directions not intended by the college. I agree; but this is not what I'm talking about. What I have in mind are cases where the change in the student's beliefs and values was precisely what some people at the college sought to produce.

Others may complain about what they regard as my narrow view of education. I disagree. I happen to believe that a good education requires the presentation of competing points of view; students should be exposed to literature that expresses these different perspectives in the words of reputable representatives of those positions. A good education is one in which students will be exposed to beliefs and values that differ from their own; it is one in which students are encouraged even to question their own beliefs, since this process is often a necessary step in discovering how strong that position is.

What is at issue here is not education, but indoctrination. According to one writer, "Indoctrination is the order of business [at many American colleges]. One historian at the University of Massachusetts begins his classes by saying: 'This course will be consistently anti-American.'"[21] I am struck by the fact that many of the Christian colleges I've been talking about don't want prospective parents and students to know that some of these things are occurring on their campuses. I talk frequently with teachers in respected Christian high schools and ask what evangelical colleges they now recommend. Increasingly, I find, the experiences of earlier graduates from their schools make it difficult for them to recommend many of the more highly regarded schools.

Some readers may have found these last few pages heavy going. If so, I apologize. But I cannot apologize for trying to draw attention to some serious problems that exist on many evangelical campuses. The evangelical college should have much to offer. But there will always be forces at work on these campuses that will, intentionally or not, support actions and policies that subvert their purposes. If my wife and I had children whose college years still lay ahead of them, we would want to know about these problems. Because of what I see as the importance of this discussion, it will be continued from a somewhat different direction in the following chapter.

EIGHT

THE EFFECT OF HIGHER EDUCATION ON RELIGIOUS FAITH

This chapter marks the beginning of a slight change in direction for this book. As before, I continue to be interested in helping Christian families select a college. But, as I've indicated several times already, one of the biggest question marks wise Christian families will have as they weigh their choices is what effect this or that college will have on the religious faith of the student. One of the things I want to show in this chapter is that there is no simple answer to this question. It is true that Christian young people have lost their faith at secular colleges; it is also true that the faith of some has been strengthened in that challenging environment. And it is also the case that Christian young people have lost their faith studying at evangelical colleges that everyone—or almost everyone—regards as "safe." This chapter, then, will examine the important question: What effect does higher education have on religious faith? In this and the following chapter, I'll also take a look at some of the specific challenges to faith that are encountered not only at secular colleges but at evangelical colleges as well. I will then suggest some resources that may be helpful in meeting these challenges.

Parents and students need to understand that there is something about the educational process itself that serves to weaken and undermine the values that students may bring to their college experience. According to James Davison Hunter, a sociologist at the University of Virginia:

> Somehow exposure to the realm of higher education weakened the grip of religious conviction over a person's life. Thus whatever religious beliefs and practices an individual carried in with him at the start of his educational sojourn would have been either seriously compromised or abandoned altogether by the time he was ready to graduate. Minimally holding on to the religion of his adolescence would have proven difficult if not impossible.[1]

Higher education does result in a movement away from the religious, moral, and cultural convictions that students have when they first enter college. Few Christian families would be surprised to learn that this is the case when young people study in secular schools. But Professor Hunter made the surprising and somewhat shocking discovery that even study in evangelical Christian colleges has this effect on students. His research in a number of leading evangelical colleges revealed that on those campuses, over time, "The traditional religious and cultural orthodoxy of conservative Protestantism is weakening."[2] The evidence he uncovered shows that such a weakening is a consequence of the educational process itself, even when the education is received in the environment of a Christian college. "Instead of buttressing the traditions in the lives of its adherents," Hunter writes, the educational process—even in Christian colleges—"undermines them."[3] Why is this so?

Well, for one thing, the period of time during which most young people go to college coincides with a period in the human life cycle when we are most susceptible to change in our beliefs and values. Our arrival at college coincides with the time in life when we make the decisions that give final shape to the worldview we will have for the rest of our lives. Hunter puts it this way:

> A good deal of research has made it clear that late adolescence and early adulthood are crucial years in terms of value formation. Attitudes and opinions coalesce into a relatively distinct world view, a world view that remains essentially intact through old age. The pursuit of higher education through this period of the life cycle adds a peculiar twist to this pattern. Attitudes and opinions change through this period but they change in a particular direction. Higher education tends to liberalize the way in which people view the world and live their lives. For example, people . . . experiment to various degrees with different life-style patterns; they even become more liberal on social, political and religious issues.[4]

In short, "Higher education produces large, pervasive, and enduring effects. The knowledge one acquires and the changes which occur in one's value orientation during this formative period in higher education are, in large part, retained."[5]

It is natural for college-age young people to doubt and question things they have always believed. This makes it especially important for them to have access to people they trust and respect who can ease those doubts and answer those questions. Many young people are especially vulnerable at this time in their lives to indoctrination by clever professors who know how to exploit the students' weaknesses.

I don't want to leave the impression that college should not have a major effect on the values of college students. I don't think much of schools that see their task only as one of reinforcing beliefs students have when they enter college. That kind of education isn't worth much. A college education ought to lead the student to think for herself, to question, to reevaluate things. What I would hope is that this process would result in the student becoming a stronger Christian in the sense that she understands better what she believes and why she believes it. Sadly, the process often produces a quite different result.

We happen to be at one of those points in the history of higher education when, it seems, a disproportionate number of professors appear interested primarily in indoctrination, in persuasion, and in converting students to their particular worldview. These attitudes, I have found, are often more characteristic of those who describe themselves as liberal. In practice, many liberals turn out to be quite illiberal toward anyone who dares to disagree with their enlightened opinions. Books that don't agree with their position are unworthy of being placed on reading lists or of being used as texts; students who fail to see the wisdom of the professor are often given lower grades, because their disagreement is perceived as a sign of ignorance or stubbornness. Fortunately, this is not always the case. But the more radical the professor, the more likely this is to be the case. And, unfortunately, there are a lot of radicals on college campuses these days.

According to one national magazine, some 10,000 American college professors freely identify themselves as Marxists. To this number can be added thousands of others who strongly sympathize with left-wing political and social values. People like this are seldom interested in treating the Christian worldview fairly.

According to Paul Hollander, a professor of sociology at the University of Massachusetts, the single major resource of left-wing culture in America is the college campus. "Even if the majority of the students in the nation today do not subscribe to [this] mentality," he writes, "large and vocal portions of their teachers do, especially in the humanities and social sciences. My own discipline, sociology, has, for example been quite thoroughly politicized and probably a majority of its practitioners take [this way of thinking] for granted."[6] His book cites many other examples of the inroads that this way of thinking has made into other academic areas.

The selection of a major area of study plays an important role in determining when students abandon beliefs and values held earlier in life. According to Hunter, the rejection of such values is "more likely to occur among students who major in the social sciences and, to a lesser extent, the humanities, while students who major in the natural sciences, business, or religious studies are less prone to these kinds of world view changes."[7]

Hunter's book is titled *Evangelicalism, The Coming Generation*. It is important to recognize that the focus of his book is not higher education in general but higher education in those evangelical Christian colleges usually regarded as the cream of the crop. His research shows that while many Christians believe that studying in such an environment strengthens the religious faith of the student, the result is often just the opposite. As we've just noted, part of this is due to the liberalizing effect any education has at this particular time in a student's life. But Hunter has discovered another, more disturbing reason why evangelical Christian colleges weaken the faith of their students. According to Hunter, there has been a serious erosion of commitment to the theological and cultural traditions of evangelicalism among many Christian college faculty. Such faculty obviously have an enormous influence on their Christian students. Because many of these students regard their professors as objects of authority and as people they want to emulate, the thinking of the faculty has a significant influence on the worldview of the students. In Hunter's words,

> In short, [Christian college] faculty overall are even less committed to the theological and cultural traditions of the

> Evangelical heritage than their students. It is difficult to imagine this fact *not* having a profound effect on the world view of students. Not surprisingly, it is faculty in the social sciences and the humanities who are more disaffected from the traditions than faculty in the arts (including the performing arts), natural sciences, and business curricula. . . . There is then, among many faculty [of Christian colleges], a sense that true and vital Christianity depends upon a debunking of many of the traditions of conservative Protestantism.[8]

Dealing with this problem is the responsibility of the trustees and administrators of the evangelical colleges involved. But, since there are few signs that these people even recognize the problem, let alone intend to do anything about it, Christian parents and students must become alert to the issue and take steps on their own to confront it.

One reason many Christian families look positively on certain religious colleges is because of what they regard as the relative safety of these schools. The Christian college is thought to insulate the Christian student from anything that threatens the integrity of his or her community. Obviously, the secular college provides no insulation at all. But because there is no insulation like this in the public university setting, Hunter points out, "religious students are continually reminded of the vulnerability of their beliefs. The threat to the plausibility of their beliefs is external and communicated. Thus mere recognition of the minority status of their convictions relative to competing perspectives appears to foster a 'fortress mentality' among the strongly committed. In this situation the believer's identity as a believer is accentuated and reinforced; his world view is [made tougher]. The Evangelical in this context becomes even 'more' Evangelical."[9] In other words, many Christian students respond to what they clearly see as the challenges to their faith on a secular campus and, in the process, become stronger Christians.

But something quite different often occurs in the setting of what is thought to be the "safe" Christian college. Here, it is very easy for students to let their guard down. "Such social environments," Hunter writes, "are perceived as safe, and thus, one's defensive posture can be relaxed; in community with others of the same view, it is possible to take one's world for granted. . . . The setting of the Evangelical college, we can infer, does allow for a relaxation of 'cognitive defenses.' Yet it is in the safety of this setting that the erosive effects of education can take place. In this case, the threat is not external and visible but internal and, by and large, unperceived."[10] It is helpful to remember in all this that James Davison Hunter is a professor of sociology at one of the most highly regarded public universities in the country. He is expressing his concern that evangelical Christian colleges often have an effect on their students that is the exact opposite of what they claim and what Christian families expect.

Several important lessons can be learned from all this. For one thing, Christian families should recognize that the effect that different kinds of colleges can have on their children's religious faith is much more complicated than many think. It is possible that attendance at a secular college could result in a strengthening of the student's faith, whereas study at a "safe" Christian college would weaken it.

Lesson number two: A key factor in how higher education affects religious faith concerns the degree to which the student is prepared and keeps her guard up. As a general rule, a properly prepared student, whose guard is up, can withstand any assault on her faith on any campus in the country. On the other hand, an improperly prepared student, or one who lets down her guard, can be led to abandon important values even at so-called Christian colleges. In fact, one thing that makes church-related colleges such a fruitful breeding ground for doubt, skepticism, and unbelief may be the fact that many students in such a setting relax their guard. After all, such students think, isn't this a "Christian" school? If I can't trust these people, whom can I trust?

Consider a situation in which precisely the same theory is presented in two different classrooms: one in a secular college and one in a "Christian" college. In the secular college, the evangelical student has his guard up. He is more attentive and hence quicker to question what he hears from a professor he believes might be biased against his faith. On the other hand, an unprepared evangelical student in a religious college—even one his parents think is soundly evangelical—tends to accept everything he hears because he believes he can trust this teacher. When that teacher shouldn't be trusted because he has been moving away from positions the Christian college is supposed to defend, the student is in an especially vulnerable position.

The question then becomes: How can students get better prepared? What can be done to help them get their guard up? Probably the most important element in getting students prepared is helping them realize that none of the challenges they'll encounter are new. It may be new to them. But somewhere—if not in their college library then in some other library or bookstore—there are books that take up those challenges and answer them.

For example, the first philosophy course I took in college presented me with such a challenge. Ironically, I took the course in an evangelical Christian college under an evangelical professor. During one of his first lectures on ancient Greek philosophy, the professor mentioned an ancient religious practice known as the *taurobolium*. During the celebration of the taurobolium, people being initiated into the cult reclined in a pit under a platform of boards on which a bull was slaughtered. As the blood of the dying bull dripped through the cracks between the boards and onto the initiates, they would often throw back

The Effect of Higher Education on Religious Faith 97

their heads to allow the blood to wet their faces, nostrils, and lips. Often, initiates would drink the hot blood. My professor referred to the ritual as a "baptism of blood" and explained that many commentators described the initiate rising from the pit as one who had died and risen with his savior-God. My professor went on to point out that when a lamb was used in place of a bull, the initiate could be said to have been "washed in the blood of the lamb." The teacher left all of us in the class with the clear impression that this ritual was commonly practiced in the Mediterranean world for centuries before the Birth of Christ. The questions that even a five-minute discussion like this can raise in the mind of a twenty-year-old student are obvious.

Because I trusted the professor, I simply accepted what he said. The pressure of my course work at the time made it impossible for me to do any research on the matter. But the professor's claims continued to trouble me, and I promised myself that someday I'd look into the whole matter more thoroughly. As it turned out, several decades were to pass before I finally turned my attention to the question of the taurobolium. What I discovered was that my trusted Christian professor was completely wrong about the most crucial claim made in his lecture. He was correct when he said that the rite of the taurobolium was common throughout the Mediterranean world; and he had described the ritual accurately. What he was totally wrong about was the period of time in which he placed the practice. I discovered that all of the historical evidence suggests that the taurobolium originated *after* the origin of Christianity. I also learned that there is good reason to believe that the pagan cults that popularized the taurobolium did so because it gave them a kind of perverse alternative to certain obvious Christian symbols at a time when Christianity was attracting many converts from those pagan religions. All of this information was readily available to my professor at the time he included the topic of the taurobolium in his lectures. I can only assume that he was passing on material he had picked up secondhand and had neglected to check out for himself.[11]

In this example, the professor simply had his facts wrong—something that is relatively easy to correct if one knows where to look. Other issues that can create problems for students are more difficult to handle since they involve complex arguments that can vex even highly trained scholars. One example of such an issue is the so-called problem of evil; it is a problem that every thinking Christian will encounter sooner or later. If God is all-powerful, it seems as though He must have the power to eliminate evil in His creation. If God is all-good, it seems to follow that He wants to eliminate evil in His creation. And if God is all-knowing, it seems as though He must know how to eliminate evil from His creation. Then why doesn't He? Why does so much evil that seems meaningless and senseless exist in a world that Christians believe was created by an all-powerful, all-good, and all-knowing God? Many Christian scholars believe that the problem of evil is the most serious challenge to religious faith. Their inability to sort through the issues has led many people to deny the power or goodness of God and led others to reject the very existence of God. This book is not an appropriate place to begin a lengthy answer to the problem of evil. What is appropriate is to point out to Christian parents and students that this is one challenge the student is bound to encounter in college. It is also relevant to point the student to some books (identified at the end of the chapter) in which he or she can get some help in dealing with this problem.

Other specific problems are likely to arise in the student's future. Some of them pertain to the relationship between science and religion. *Is the theory of evolution true?* is one such question. *Are miracles possible?* is another. I know of no serious problem that arises out of the supposed conflict between science and religion that hasn't been dealt with adequately in one book or another. At the end of this chapter, I'll mention a few of these books.

Many college students are confused by their first exposure to the various forms of biblical criticism. They are totally unprepared when they first learn about methods like form criticism and redaction criticism. It is natural to assume that, when their professors describe "the assured results" of these methods, the teachers must know what they're talking about. Once again, it is important to know that there are places to turn for help.

What I've provided in the last few pages are examples of some specific problems or challenges that the student will undoubtedly encounter early in his or her college program. What I've said is that, whether it is one of these difficulties or some other problem, the student needs to know that she is not on her own. Reputable scholars have thought through these issues and provided a record of their work in books. When troubled by a problem, the wise student will seek help in locating those books and use them as guides in thinking through the difficulty.

At the end of this chapter and the next, I will identify some books that deal with these problems. The books identified at the end of this chapter deal with some of the more specific problems that students may encounter in college. The books mentioned at the end of chapter nine evaluate more general systems of thought.

Suggested Reading for Problems Mentioned in this Chapter:

The Problem of Evil:
C. S. Lewis, *The Problem of Pain* (New York: Macmillan, 1962).

Ronald Nash, *Faith and Reason: Searching for a Rational Faith* (Grand Rapids: Zondervan, 1988).

C. Stephen Evans, *Philosophy of Religion* (Downers Grove, Il.: InterVarsity, 1985).

The Problem of Miracles:
C. S. Lewis, *Miracles* (New York: Macmillan, 1947).
Ronald Nash, *Faith and Reason: Searching for a Rational Faith* (Grand Rapids: Zondervan, 1988).
C. Stephen Evans, *The Quest for Faith* (Downers Grove, Il.: InterVarsity, 1986).

Biblical Criticism:
Ronald Nash, *Christian Faith and Historical Understanding* (Grand Rapids: Zondervan, 1984).
D. A. Carson and John D. Woodbridge, editors, *Scripture and Truth* (Grand Rapids: Zondervan, 1983).
F. F. Bruce, *Are the New Testament Documents Reliable?* (Grand Rapids: Eerdmans, 1960).
R. K. Harrison, *Biblical Criticism: Historical, Literary, and Textual* (Grand Rapids: Zondervan, 1978).

Science and Religion (including evolution):
Charles Hummel, *The Galileo Connection* (Downers Grove, Il.: InterVarsity, 1986).
Richard Bube, *The Human Quest,* (Waco, Texas: Word, 1971)—out of print.[12]
Bernard Ramm, *A Christian View of Science and Scripture* (Grand Rapids: Eerdmans, 1955).
Donald McKay, *Science and the Quest for Meaning* (Grand Rapids: Eerdmans, 1982)—out of print.

Other Issues:
Ronald Nash, *Christianity and the Hellenistic World* (Grand Rapids: Zondervan, 1984).
Ronald Nash, *The Concept of God* (Grand Rapids: Zondervan, 1983).

NINE

SOME THINGS TO PREPARE FOR

There is no way that Christians can deal responsibly with the variety of competing religious and secular alternatives to Christianity in the academic marketplace without information. To attempt a response without information is like a soldier's going into battle without weapons. The sad thing about Christians who try to do battle with alien theories is that the information they need is already available. All the Christian needs is guidance about where to look for it.

I have already recommended some books that can serve as a starting point for anyone dealing with a few specific problems. By the time this chapter is finished, I will have identified a number of other books that discuss entire systems of thinking that are at odds with Christianity. I do not recommend dumping ten or twenty books on any high school senior or college freshman who, at the moment, happens to be uninterested in this or that subject. That would be counterproductive. But it does help to know which books are relevant so that when the student admits to being puzzled or troubled by something, the parent has something to put in her hands. It is one thing, however, for a parent to suggest that a student read a particular book; it is another thing for the parent herself to have read the book first so as to be able to discuss it and the student's problem.

The Importance of Thinking in Terms of Worldviews

Instead of viewing Christianity as a collection of theological bits and pieces to be believed or debated, Christians should approach it as a total world- and life-view. Once they understand that both Christianity and its competitors are worldviews, they will be in a better position to judge Christianity's strengths with respect to other systems.

A worldview is a conceptual scheme by which we, consciously or unconsciously, place or fit everything we believe. We use our worldview to interpret and judge reality. Unfortunately, many people have little or no idea what a worldview is, or even that they have one. One of the more important things a good education can do for students is to help them realize what a worldview is, assist them in achieving a better understanding of their own worldview, and aid them in improving their worldview. From an informed Christian perspective, this education in worldviews can be done best in the setting of a Christian college.

The right eyeglasses can put the world into clearer focus. The correct worldview can function in much the same way. When someone looks at the world through the wrong worldview, the world won't make much sense, or what the person thinks makes sense will be wrong in important respects. Viewing the world through the correct worldview can have important repercussions for the rest of a person's beliefs.

The case for or against Christianity should be evaluated in terms of total systems. The reason why many people reject Christianity is not due to their problems with one or two isolated issues; it results rather for the simple reason that their anti-Christian worldview leads them to reject information and arguments that provide believers with important support for the Christian worldview.

Christianity is not simply a religion that tells human beings how they may be forgiven and enter into fellowship with the holy, personal, sovereign, and triune God. Christianity is also a total world- and life-view. Because so many elements of a worldview are philosophical in nature, Christians need to become more conscious of the importance of philosophy. Though philosophy and religion often use different languages and often arrive at different conclusions, they deal with the same questions: What exists? (metaphysics); how should human beings live? (ethics); how do humans know? (epistemology); and so on. Philosophy matters because the Christian worldview has an intrinsic connection to philosophy and the world of ideas. It matters because philosophy is related in a critically important way to life, culture, and religion. And it matters because the systems opposing Christianity use philosophical methods and arguments. One book that can introduce students to philosophy in general and to thinking about worldviews in particular is a recent book titled *Faith and Reason: Searching for a Rational Faith*.[1] The book also takes a detailed look at various arguments that are thought to make belief in the existence of God rational. It discusses the problem of evil, the most serious challenge to religious faith; the possibility of miracles, such as the Resurrection of Christ; and the possibility of life after death.

The Christian student, who understands what the Christian worldview is and who recognizes the philosophical superiority of this worldview to its competitors, has taken one important step—perhaps the most important step—toward being prepared for the intellectual challenges to her faith that she'll encounter in college.

In the rest of this chapter, I will identify some of the major contemporary enemies of the Christian worldview. I'll begin with systems that one is likely to encounter only on secular campuses or at liberal denominational colleges. Somewhere along the line, we will find that I am talking about theories and systems of thought that also have their advocates on evangelical Christian campuses. It is not my purpose to give lengthy expositions of these positions or to answer them. That would require a longer and different kind of book than this. Rather, my goal is to identify the enemy and direct the student to a few of the many books that provide the necessary and longer discussions. This list of books appears at the end of the chapter.

Naturalism

The major competition to the Christian worldview, in the part of the world normally thought of as Christendom, is a system that often goes by the name of *Naturalism*. The basic claim of Naturalism is that "Nothing exists outside the material, mechanical, natural order."

For naturalists, the universe is a closed, self-explanatory system. The naturalist's universe is analogous to a box. Everything that happens inside the box is caused by or is explainable in terms of other things that exist within the box. Nothing (including God) exists outside the box; therefore, nothing outside the box we call the universe or nature can have any causal effect within the box.

Given such a worldview, it is small wonder that people who are naturalists object to major elements of the Christian worldview. Any naturalist is precluded from believing in God, spirit, soul, angels, miracles, prayer, providence, immortality, heaven, sin, and salvation, as Christians normally understand these notions, for one simple reason: Such beliefs are logically incompatible with the naturalist's worldview.

It is important to notice that no naturalist ever bothers to prove that Naturalism is true. Indeed, as more than one book argues, it is impossible to prove the truth of Naturalism. The commitment that some people make to a system like Naturalism is similar in important respects to the commitment that other people make to Christianity. It is important to realize, therefore, that the naturalist, who claims that miracles are impossible, is not somehow more in tune with modern science. His rejection of miracles—however hard he attempts to dress it up—is a reflection of his ultimate religious commitment to a naturalistic worldview.[2]

Humanism

Humanism is a word more used than understood. It is a term with many meanings, some quite acceptable. For example, anyone who believes in the importance and value of the human person could be said to be a humanist. The Humanism I have in view is something quite different. One way to define this anti-Christian Humanism is to let its advocates speak for themselves:

> Humanists regard the universe as self-existing and not created.
> Humanism asserts that the nature of the universe depicted by modern science makes unacceptable any supernatural cosmic guarantees of human value.
> Religious humanism considers the complete realization of human personality to be the end of man's life and seeks its development and fulfillment in the here and now.
> In the place of the old attitudes involved in worship and prayer the humanist finds his religious emotions expressed in a heightened sense of personal life and in a cooperative effort to promote social well-being.
> Man is at last becoming aware that he alone is responsible for the realization of the world of his dreams, that he has within himself the power for its achievement.[3]

The Humanism described in these claims is a religion without God. Or to put it another way, it is a religion in which humankind assumes the place of God. Humanism is, in the words of an ancient Greek philosopher, the belief that Man (and not God) is the measure or standard of all things. While contemporary Humanism is often opposed to organized religion, it can also assume religious forms. For example, various manifestations of the so-called New Age Movement are simply religious, anti-Christian, variants of Humanism.

Marxism

In its classic form, Marxism was a form of Naturalism. Karl Marx was clearly a naturalist who denied the existence of any nonmaterial reality that could create, control, or influence the natural order. Marx believed that all aspects of human life (including philosophy, religion, art, politics, and science) are determined by the ways in which human beings make a living.

This is not the place to discuss Marx's writings, the variations of Marxism offered by later thinkers like Lenin, or the innumerable interpretations and theories set forth by the mass of Marxists running around college campuses in the nations of the West. It is ironic that there are few, if any, serious Marxists left in nations like the Soviet Union, mainland China, East Germany, and other nations still captive to the power of the Red Army and the caprice of their nonelected rulers. The real game in such countries—apart from all the old rhetoric about things like the proletariat and the class struggle—is how these nonelected rulers can retain their power. Perhaps there is another game going on as well: how these rulers can stop the economic bleeding caused by the repeated failures of their socialist systems.

But while the oppressed and suffering citizens of Marxist

nations long for the freedom of the West, benighted "intellectuals" in the West continue to tell college students how evil nations like America are in comparison with the Soviet Union. And while Marxist states, like mainland China and the U.S.S.R., finally acknowledge the failure of socialism and turn increasingly in the direction of capitalist incentives,[4] western intellectuals continue to urge their nations to abandon capitalism for the kind of socialism that has brought Marxist states to the brink of economic ruin. For many of these individuals, Karl Marx has become the prophet of a new religion whose writings must be scrutinized with all the devotion and passion that Christians used to bring to their study of the Bible. The semi-religious faith of these Marxists has no essential link to reality. It is difficult to think of one nontrivial claim made by Marx that has not been falsified.

As irrational as all this may be, the student who is put in a position where she has to answer some Marxist professor will have to master a great deal of literature and a lot of complex theories and arguments. For the purpose of this book, I must content myself with urging the student not to get taken in by all the hoopla. The reading list at the end of the chapter suggests a couple of relatively simple books that can serve as a starting point for a critically informed understanding of Marxism. Separate reading lists in these books will direct the reader to other studies. Later in this chapter, I briefly discuss a movement known as Liberation Theology, which is a form of Marxism that is frequently encountered these days on Christian college campuses.

Eastern Mysticism

On many college campuses, especially schools on the West coast, the pantheistic mysticism of various Eastern religions is popular among students and faculty. One feature of this mysticism is the claim that "God" (or ultimate reality or whatever) lies beyond the limits of human knowledge. Hence we must seek the ultimate in the inner depths of our own being. For some, this search is helped by the use of drugs.

There are too many versions of this way of thinking to discuss in detail. Some of them, like Transcendental Meditation, attempt to hide behind various disguises. There seems little need to do much reading in this area until one is actually in a setting where this kind of thinking has to be dealt with. I should warn you that, because of the nature of these views, their advocates are not moved by appeals to logic or reason. The highest "truth," they feel, is beyond or above human reason. Ironically, these same people reject Christianity because, they say, it is so "unreasonable." One of the interesting things about college is the really strange people you can meet.

New Age Movements

If any movement can lay claim to being chic these days, it is the New Age thinking that nationally known personalities like Shirley MacLaine have brought so much attention to. Actually, Eastern mysticism is one of the sources of New Age thinking. It also includes—depending on the form it takes—elements of reincarnation, spiritism, along with other beliefs and practices of pagan religions long thought to be dead. New Age religions are especially dangerous to uninformed Christians because they frequently use Christian language and symbols with thoroughly inverted meanings. Some New Age advocates talk reverently about Jesus but regard Him as simply another prophet of New Age consciousness. Some use the Bible but twist the meaning of the Scriptures outrageously to suit their anti-Christian convictions. It's probably a good idea to have a book or two on this subject in the collection of books you take to college.

Neo-Orthodoxy

I now turn my attention to a number of theories and systems that can be encountered on the campuses of evangelical Christian colleges. Of course, they will also be found at secular and religiously liberal schools as well. The growing presence of these positions within the evangelical college movement reflects, among other things, an inattention to sound doctrine at some of these schools. This is often a problem within denominations that stress religious experience over such equally important things as systematic theology. I taught philosophy and religion at an evangelical college affiliated with such a denomination early in my career. I attempted without success to get the administration to add courses in Christian doctrine that would help students to think about their beliefs in a systematic way. I still have the distinct impression that the administration of the college was afraid of courses like this. Perhaps they feared that systematic thinking about the Christian faith would detract from the college's desired emphasis upon personal piety and holiness. I sometimes thought they were afraid that systematic thinking about Christian doctrine might lead some students to become Calvinists! Whatever their reason, systematic theology was never made an option for students at the school. Of course, thirty years ago the religion faculty at that college was theologically conservative. It is interesting to note, however, how the theological climate at many Arminian, experience-oriented, colleges has changed. This is true of schools affiliated with the Church of the Nazarene, the Church of God (Anderson, Indiana), Oral Roberts University and other pentecostal schools, a number of schools in the Wesleyan/Holiness tradition, and many Baptist colleges.

Many of these schools now tolerate the attitude toward the Bible known as Neo-orthodoxy. You should realize that Neo-orthodoxy is a complicated movement. But the major element of the position that I'm talking about is its refusal to recognize the Bible as the revealed Word of God. Professors who are under the influence of Neo-orthodoxy want students to believe that the Bible (which they sometimes describe as a totally human and fallible book) *becomes* the Word of God under certain circumstances. We must never, they insist, confuse the Bible with the Word of God. The Word of God is what God says to us "in our hearts" when we read the Bible or have religious experiences. It is this inner, totally subjective experience that no one can fully share with any other person that is the Word of God. The Bible is only an instrument—perhaps one of many that God uses—to confront us with the Word of God.

James Davison Hunter does a nice job of explaining what is at stake in the Neo-orthodox approach to the Bible:

> Where Evangelicalism argued that the Bible itself in its original form is the unerring Word of God, neo-orthodoxy argues that the Bible "becomes" the Word of God. It is only when the individual reads or hears the Scriptures through the eyes and ears of faith that the text becomes the Word of God. What is more, neo-orthodoxy has devalued the historicity of the biblical account of historical events. The crucial issue from this standpoint is not that these events actually occured but simply that God is trying to teach us something of spiritual significance by the symbolism of these stories. Thus, for example, the believer does not have to be concerned whether or not the origin of the world occurred precisely in the manner described in the Book of Genesis. What is central is that the believer learns from this that, among other things, God is the source and creator of life. In its logical extreme, this form of theologizing would conclude that it is unimportant whether the Resurrection of Christ actually occurred, but merely that God is teaching the believer something of tremendous importance by this story.[5]

Neo-orthodox thinkers either do not believe or do not understand the notion of revealed truth. If the Bible is not a divine communication of revealed truth, the whole question of the Bible's truth becomes insignificant. Why worry then if some college professor claims to have found errors in the Bible. It isn't the Bible that's important any more; what is important is the inward, subjective religious experience we have when reading the Bible.

Like every issue discussed in this chapter, this is a complicated problem that does not lend itself easily to a short discussion. But because there is such a strong possibility that this view will be encountered at the Christian college you attend—if that is your choice—it is wise to be prepared on this issue. The reading list at the end of the chapter will direct you to a more complete treatment of the whole matter. Be on the watch for professors who claim that the Bible is not the Word of God but only *becomes* the Word of God under certain conditions.

Liberation Theology

Once again, we have a complex movement whose adherents don't often tell the whole story. Put in the simplest possible terms, Liberation theology is a movement that downplays the historic, doctrinal side of Christianity and emphasizes instead the importance of Christian action *(praxis)* on behalf of poor and oppressed people. Liberation theology can appear very attractive to dedicated Christian students, who find it easy to identify with the underdogs of the world. And what group of underdogs deserves compassion and help more than the poor and oppressed?

As I said at the beginning of this section, many proponents of Liberation theology are effective propagandists for their movement. And, as we know, propaganda and full disclosure are often two entirely different things. Advocates of Liberation theology, especially on evangelical college campuses, would have their audiences believe that liberationism is nothing more than a call to socially concerned Christians to become active on behalf of poor and oppressed peoples. I don't know anyone who objects to this.[6]

One thing liberation thinkers try to cover over is that their emphasis on action and their de-emphasis on sound Christian doctrine has brought many of them to the brink of theological heresy. Many Roman Catholic liberation theologians have been condemned by the Vatican for denying the Christian Church's historic understanding of such essential Christian beliefs as the atonement and resurrection of Christ. Many Protestant liberation thinkers are heretical in similar ways.[7]

In addition to their abandonment of important Christian beliefs, most liberation theologians are Marxists of one type or another. In many cases, their Marxism leads them to support violent, Marxist revolutions. Several critics of the movement have pointed out that Liberation theology has been misnamed. Its distortion or rejection of the Christian Gospel means that it cannot offer human beings liberation from sin. Its frequent disinterest in democracy means that it cannot offer liberation from tyranny. And its obsession with the bad economics of socialism means that it cannot offer liberation from poverty.[8]

Many readers would be surprised to see a list of all the evangelical colleges where some variety of Christian Marxism is not only taught, but strongly advocated. Theologically informed Christians will resist the movement's twisting of the Gospel to suit its political agenda. Economically literate Christians will unmask the movement's bad economics that can only make the plight of poor people worse. And finally, every Christian should criticize the movement's love affair with corrupt Third World dictators like Fidel Castro. Fortunately, there is a growing body of literature available on this subject.

Process Theology

Of all the systems mentioned in this chapter, Process theology is without question the most difficult to understand.

Even harder to understand is why any evangelical would think this system has anything to offer the Christian. As its name suggests, Process theology begins with the assumption that all of reality (including God) is characterized by change or process. Many process thinkers argue that there are serious problems with a classical view of God that emphasizes God's immutability or unchangeableness. A God who is incapable of change, they say, cannot be the loving and caring God of the Bible. As the books cited at the end of this chapter point out, this line of argument depends on a calculated disregard of some important distinctions.

Scholars who are sympathetic to Process theology often accept different versions of the system. In its most extreme forms, Process theology has more in common with Buddhism than with Christianity. Process thinkers at this end of the line deny the sovereignty of God; God's power is limited. This is seen, for example, in their rejection of the biblical doctrine of Creation. God did not create the world, they teach. Rather, God and the world have always existed. Even worse from a biblical standpoint, they claim that God needs the world, just as the world needs God. God and the world are interdependent and co-eternal dimensions of reality. Nonevangelical process thinkers make clear their rejection of such important Christian doctrines as the Incarnation, the Atonement, and the Resurrection. Evangelicals who are attracted to process thought may find it only a matter of time before they are willing to sacrifice these essential elements of the Christian faith on the altar of their favorite philosophical system.

It should be obvious that when any thinker denies the doctrines of the Incarnation, the Resurrection, or Creation, he or she has moved beyond the limits of biblical Christianity—even though he or she may be a professor in a Christian school. Some evangelicals who are committed to the process system refuse (or claim to refuse) to go this far. When this is the case, what gives them away is their denial that God knows the future, another tenet of this system. In fact, it is this denial of God's knowledge of the future that seems to account for the system's popularity with many Arminians. They are so anxious to secure an area of free choice for human beings that they are even willing to impose limits on God's knowledge and power. This may explain the growing influence of Process theology at colleges that are Holiness, or Wesleyan, in their theology. Process thought can be found at some Nazarene colleges, at Anderson College, at several Baptist schools, and even at an institution like Azusa Pacific University.

Because of the movement's complexity, none of the literature about it is especially easy to read. But, as one of the books cited at the end of this chapter makes clear, Process theology is a movement that is incompatible with historic Christianity.

Conclusion

I have said repeatedly that properly prepared Christian students can attend college anywhere without that school having an adverse effect on the student's religious faith. Proper preparation, however, is impossible if one does not know or cannot recognize what to look for. The preparation that is required does not mean that every student has to become an expert in theology, apologetics, biblical studies, philosophy, and non-Christian religions. But, it certainly helps to have had an introduction to the subject of worldviews. It also helps when the student can recognize a naturalist, humanist, Marxist, or process thinker when she sees one. And, when that student finds herself challenged by one of the problems I discussed in the last chapter or by one of the systems I've described in this chapter, it helps if she knows where she can go for some answers.

Some readers may find that this book has made their choice of a college far more difficult than they expected it to be. After all, I have pointed out what few people have been willing to state publicly, namely, that some evangelical Christian colleges have serious theological problems on their campuses. I have also drawn attention to the fact that it is sometimes easier for students to go wrong spiritually and theologically at supposedly evangelical colleges than at many secular schools. I see no reason to cover over this fact. But, I repeat: Properly prepared Christian students can attend college anywhere without that school having an adverse effect on the student's religious faith.

Christian families should not assume that just because some of the colleges on their list are evangelical schools with familiar and respected names, there is no need for them to investigate those schools carefully. Perhaps, if more families let the people who run these schools know that the cat is out of the bag, the colleges would begin the long overdue task of returning the schools to long forgotten standards.

Suggested Reading for Systems Mentioned in this Chapter:

The Nature of Worldviews and the Christian Worldview:
    Ronald Nash, *Faith and Reason: Searching for a Rational Faith* (Grand Rapids: Zondervan, 1988).
    James W. Sire, *The Universe Next Door* (Downers Grove, Il.: InterVarsity, 1988).

Naturalism:
    Ronald Nash, *Faith and Reason: Searching for a Rational Faith* (Grand Rapids: Zondervan, 1988).

Humanism:
    James Hitchcock, *What is Secular Humanism?* (Ann Arbor, Mi.: Servant Books, 1982).

Marxism:
    Klaus Bockmuehl, *The Challenge of Marxism* (Colorado Springs: Holmers and Howard, 1988).
    Sidney Hook, editor, *Marx and the Marxists* (Princeton, New Jersey: D. Van Nostrand, 1955).
    Ronald Nash, *Poverty and Wealth* (Westchester, Il.: Crossway Books, 1986).

Eastern Mysticism:
    Norman Anderson, *Christianity and World Religions* (Downers Grove, Il.: InterVarsity Press, 1984).
    James W. Sire, *The Universe Next Door* (Downers Grove, Il.: InterVarsity Press, 1988).

New Age Movements:
    Douglas Groothuis, *Unmasking the New Age* (Downers Grove, Il.: InterVarsity Press, 1986).
    Douglas Groothuis, *Confronting the New Age* (Downers Grove, Il.: InterVarsity Press, 1988).

Neo-orthodoxy:
    Ronald Nash, *Christian Faith and Historical Understanding* (Grand Rapids: Zondervan, 1983).
    Ronald Nash, *The Word of God and the Mind of Men* (Grand Rapids: Zondervan, 1982).

Liberation Theology:
    Humberto Belli and Ronald Nash, editors, *Beyond Liberation Theology*, forthcoming.
    Ronald Nash, editor, *Liberation Theology* (Grand Rapids: Baker, 1988).
    Ronald Nash, *Poverty and Wealth* (Westchester, Il.: Crossway Books, 1986).
    Ronald Nash, *Social Justice and the Christian Church* (Grand Rapids: Baker, 1987).

Process Theology:
  Ronald Nash, *The Concept of God* (Grand Rapids: Zondervan, 1983).
  Ronald Nash, editor, *Process Theology* (Grand Rapids: Baker, 1987).

TEN

A CHAPTER JUST FOR STUDENTS

Even though many of the things I've said in this book appear to be directed to your parents, you really are the reason I've written it. Throughout my writing of the book, I've found it helpful to picture myself as a guest in your family's living room. Now I'd like both of us to imagine that your parents have left the room and I'm talking to you alone. What I want to say is divided into three parts. I begin by asking two important questions.

Two Questions

Are You a Christian?

Are you a Christian in the New Testament sense of the word? I trust you know that no one is a Christian because his or her parents are. Nor is anyone a Christian because he or she is a member of a church or has gone through some religious ritual like baptism. We become Christians only when, first, we know that Jesus, the Son of God, died for our sins and rose from the dead as proof that, someday, all who believe in Him will also be delivered from death (see 1 Corinthians 15). Then we must act on that knowledge and accept Jesus as our Savior and Lord (see

Romans 10:9–10). If you're not certain about your relationship to Jesus, talk to someone who can help you.

What Do You Want to Do?

As a Christian, what do you want to do with your life? The Bible teaches that the life of a Christian is not his own. We have been redeemed, bought with a price. Thus, our life belongs to the One who redeemed us (see 1 Corinthians 6:20 and Romans 12:1–2). If you want your life to count for God, then your choice of a college must be seen in the light of your total life-commitment to His will. Perhaps God wants you to serve Him in some type of full-time Christian service; perhaps He wants you to serve Him in the business world or as a computer programmer or a teacher. Don't think of college only as a means to achieve certain selfish goals; see it, rather, as a necessary step in preparing for the life-work that God wants you to perform. Keep God's will and His call before you as you make your decision.

Ten Pieces of Advice

There are lots of things I'd like to say to Christian young people as they enter college. I'll limit myself to ten brief pieces of advice.

1) Don't keep your problems and difficulties to yourself. Lots of people are in a position to help you and want to be of assistance. But they can't if they remain uninformed about your difficulties. If you run into questions for which you have no answers, the worst mistake you can make is to assume that there are no answers. One of the things I've stressed throughout this book is that nothing you encounter at college is really new. Other people have been down the same road before you, have confronted the same challenges, and have won. Somewhere the answer you're seeking and the help you need is available. Keep

the lists of books I've provided throughout this book handy and use those books when it becomes necessary.

2) Don't be a loner. There is absolutely no reason why any Christian has to feel isolated while in college—in *any* college. Here are some tips for finding new Christian friends. First, take advantage of the Bible-believing churches in your new community. Don't just visit as a stranger on Sunday morning. Attend the Sunday school class for people your age. If the first church you attend doesn't have what you're seeking, then keep looking. When you finally find what looks like a suitable church home for you, make an appointment with the pastor. Ask if he can provide information about Christian campus organizations, such as InterVarsity or the Navigators. Whatever you do, make sure you begin to fellowship with Christians whose company you enjoy.

3) Be careful about the company you keep. The Apostle Paul gave some good advice on this matter: "Do not be misled," he wrote. "Bad company corrupts good character" (1 Corinthians 15:33). No matter where you attend college, you'll have choices to make about your companions. Don't gravitate in the direction of people whose conduct and character are questionable. Nor, I trust, will you be the kind of person who has a negative effect on those who befriend you.

4) Be alert to challenges to your faith from teachers and students. Throughout this book, I've described some of the intellectual challenges you'll face. Reread those chapters every so often and remember their suggestions about other books to read.

5) Be faithful in your private devotions. Don't get to the point where you foolishly think that daily Bible reading and communion with God in prayer are somehow beneath you now that you've reached the exalted status of college student.

6) Watch for cults. There are some religious groups you can encounter at college that you should be careful of. Until you get

grounded, I suggest that you stick with known ministries, such as InterVarsity, Navigators, and Campus Crusade. Ask your parents and pastor about any groups you may have doubts about. You probably already know about cults like the Jehovah's Witnesses and the Mormons. But there are cults that may be more difficult to identify. One sign of such groups is the total domination the leaders seek to acquire over the lives, time, and money of their followers. One helpful book in this regard is *A Guide to Cults and New Religions* by Ronald Enroth and others (Downers Grove, Il.: InterVarsity Press, 1983).

7) Watch for special teachers on your campus. During one of my first years as a professor, I found an especially interested student taking some of my classes. While these were advanced courses designed primarily for philosophy majors, he wasn't a major in this area. One day, he told me why he was taking my courses. In his opinion, the faculty of this particular college at that particular time was rather undistinguished. Since he was stuck at that school, he decided that one way he could improve his education was to keep alert for news about what he called "hot" teachers, by which he meant teachers who had more to offer than the run-of-the-mill professor on that campus. I certainly have no intention of suggesting that his assessment of my courses was correct, but I do applaud his attitude and the effort he exerted to turn even a mediocre setting into a better college experience.

8) Be on the watch for professors who share your faith. At my state university, for example, a group of thirty to forty Christian professors regularly place a full page ad in the student newspaper. The ad lists their names and departments, identifies them as Christians, and invites interested students to visit them. If you have a chance, try to take courses from such people; get to know them personally. In some cases, you may make a friend for life.

9) If you make a mistake and get in the wrong class (for

you), there are times when it may be best to drop the course. But don't miss the college deadlines and get a failing grade. If, at the first class, you sense you're in the presence of a teacher you're going to have problems with, see if you can possibly get the same course from a different teacher. If things get too bad after you've passed the deadline for changing a course, dropping the course may be an option to consider. However, this should be done infrequently and only after consulting with your family.

10) If you discover that you've picked the wrong college, it may be better to transfer to a different school than languish in the wrong environment for four, long years. But once again, pay attention to the rules of the college. It is certainly better to complete a semester, earn your credits, and transfer them to the new school, than it is to drop out in the middle of a semester and lose whatever work, time, and money you've already invested. Every year, I have students who simply leave school without going through the proper withdrawal procedures. These students end up with automatic F's for all their courses that semester. In case they later decide to transfer, those F's will follow them to the new college.

Some Lessons From Scripture

I want to close this book by drawing your attention to several verses of Scripture that are relevant to your situation today and that will continue to apply in the years to come. The first of these passages is Matthew 7:24–27:

> Therefore everyone who hears these words of mine and puts them into practice is like a wise man who built his house on the rock. The rain came down, the streams rose, and the winds blew and beat against that house; yet it did not fall, because it had its foundation on the rock. But everyone who hears these words of mine and does not put them into prac-

tice is like a foolish man who built his house on sand. The rain came down, the streams rose, and the winds blew and beat against that house, and it fell with a great crash.

Do you see the point here? People whose lives are built on the right foundation are better able to stand up to whatever storms may come along in their lives. Lots of college kids leave home with high hopes and then mess up their lives with immorality and drugs. Lots of Christian kids lose their faith in college. A major reason why things like this happen is because their lives weren't grounded on the proper foundation. The apostle Paul tells us that this foundation is Jesus Christ (see 1 Corinthians 3:11). But it is certainly in the spirit of Matthew 7 to point out the importance of anything that can give us a better and stronger foundation during our college years. Getting prepared for the questions and challenges you'll be facing can be an important part of this foundation.

First Peter 5:8 also contains some good advice: "Be self-controlled and alert. Your enemy the devil prowls around like a roaring lion looking for someone to devour. Resist him, standing firm in the faith . . ." Don't think of college as a vacation; look on it as an adventure. You will be tested; your mind will be tested; your faith will be tested; your character will be tested. Approach these tests determined that you're going to come through victorious as a Christian.

The last Scripture passage I'll be quoting is a long one. It's found in Ephesians 6:10–18:

> Finally, be strong in the Lord and in his mighty power. Put on the full armor of God so that you can take your stand against the devil's schemes. For our struggle is not against flesh and blood, but against the rulers, against the authorities, against the powers of this dark world and against the spiritual forces of evil in the heavenly realms. Therefore put on the full armor of God, so that when the day of evil comes,

you may be able to stand your ground, and after you have done everything, to stand. Stand firm then, with the belt of truth buckled around your waist, with the breastplate of righteousness in place, and with your feet fitted with the readiness that comes from the gospel of peace. In addition to all this, take up the shield of faith, with which you can extinguish all the flaming arrows of the evil one. Take the helmet of salvation and the sword of the Spirit, which is the word of God. And pray in the Spirit on all occasions with all kinds of prayers and requests.

There is a lot in this passage. Consider just the following points. (1) You are part of a conflict that is often not visible to the human eye. (2) God has provided everything you'll need to come through this struggle successfully. (3) But to do this, you must put on the armor, the protection, that God has provided. (4) Be sure to stand firm; don't waver; don't let someone knock you off your feet. (5) Remember that the first element of God's armor is truth.

You don't have to be afraid of any truth in any field since God Himself is the author of all truth. Don't think that you have to run from science or philosophy or anything else in order to protect your faith. All truth is God's truth. (6) Then, remember the breastplate of righteousness. The battle ahead of you is not only an intellectual one. You're not going to do well in this conflict if your character and moral life fall short of God's standards. (7) Confidence in the Gospel gives us ability to act and move. (8) Your faith in Christ is a shield that can protect you from whatever arrows are shot in your direction. (9) The helmet of salvation is an important part of your armor. If you have doubts about your salvation, your enemy will exploit the openings that these doubts give him. (10) Never ignore the sword of the Spirit. Study God's inspired Word. Let the truth of that Word give you guidance, encouragement, and wisdom. (11) Finally, pray in the Spirit. Keep your lines of communication with God open. Share your fears and needs with Him on a regular basis and let Him demonstrate His power as He answers your prayers.

Conclusion

My task in this book is now finished. I can't think of another important thing to share with you. I would remind you of one thing Paul mentions in the Ephesians 6 passage. Remember that when he identifies the pieces of armor that God makes available to all Christians, the thing he places first is the belt of *truth*. There is no substitute for the acquisition of knowledge; there is no substitute for hard work and hard study. It's a shame when any Christian thinks that the pursuit of knowledge is somehow incompatible with a proper spiritual life. Don't fall into that trap. Of course, it is also sad when Christian young people embark on the pursuit of knowledge and, along the way, make the mistake of thinking that they no longer need the church or the Bible or the Lord. Don't fall into that trap either.

APPENDIX

SOME EVANGELICAL CHRISTIAN COLLEGES

In an effort to be helpful, this appendix will identify and provide some information about approximately sixty evangelical colleges. I want to make it clear that my inclusion of a college in this list does not constitute an endorsement, any more than my exclusion of a college indicates any reservation on my part. The colleges are grouped alphabetically by state. I then supply, when available, five items of information. Line (1) states whether the college is in fellowship with a particular denomination or whether it is interdenominational. Line (2) reports approximately how many undergraduate students the college has. Line (3) reports the college's tuition and fees for the 1988-89 school year. Other costs, including room and board, must be added to this figure. Line (4) reports the percentage of freshmen applicants accepted by the college in recent years. This number may suggest how easy or difficult it is to be admitted to the school. It may also say something about the general quality of the student body. Line (5) indicates the percentage of entering students who actually graduated from the college. A higher number may indicate general satisfaction among the student body with their college experience that encourages them to stay at the school. A lower number may point to a greater than normal dissatisfaction with the school.

There are also several Canadian schools listed at the very end of this appendix for those who might want to consider that option.

John Brown University, Siloam Springs, Arkansas 72761
   1) Interdenominational
   2) 800 students
   3) $4,145
   4) 66% of freshmen applicants accepted
   5) 35% of entering freshmen graduate

Azusa Pacific University, Azusa, California 91702
   1) Interdenominational; school's theological emphasis is Holiness
   2) 1,500 students
   3) $7,160
   4) 96% of freshmen applicants accepted
   5) 66% of entering freshmen graduate

Biola University, 13800 Biola Avenue, La Mirada, California 90639
   1) Interdenominational; one theological emphasis is dispensationalism
   2) 1,900 students
   3) $7,296
   4) 54% of freshmen applicants accepted
   5) 65% of entering freshmen graduate

The Master's College, Newhall, California 91322
   1) Independent Baptist; one theological emphasis is dispensationalism
   2) 550 students
   3) $4,950

4) 88% of freshmen applicants accepted
5) 40% of entering freshmen graduate

Point Loma Nazarene College, San Diego, California 92106
1) Church of the Nazarene; one theological emphasis is Holiness
2) 1,600 students
3) $5,925
4) 71% of freshmen applicants accepted
5) 26% of entering freshmen graduate

Simpson College, 801 Silver Avenue, San Francisco, California 94134
1) Christian and Missionary Alliance
2) 200 students
3) $4,904
4) 95% of freshmen applicants accepted
5) not available

Southern California College, Costa Mesa, California 92626
1) Assemblies of God; theological emphasis is pentecostal
2) 850 students
3) $5,402
4) 88% of freshmen applicants accepted
5) 30% of entering freshmen graduate

Westmont College, Santa Barbara, California 93108
1) Interdenominational
2) 1,200 students
3) $8,670
4) 74% of freshmen applicants accepted
5) 38% of entering freshmen graduate

Colorado Christian College, Lakewood, Colorado 80226
1) Interdenominational
2) 350 students

3) $4,680
4) 64% of freshmen applicants accepted
5) not available

Warner Southern College, Lake Wales, Florida 33853
1) Church of God (Anderson, Indiana)
2) 300 students
3) $4,670
4) 39% of freshmen applicants accepted
5) 30% of entering freshmen graduate

Northwest Nazarene College, Nampa, Idaho 83651
1) Church of the Nazarene; Holiness emphasis
2) 1,000 students
3) $5,091
4) 81% of freshmen applicants accepted
5) 30% of entering freshmen graduate

Greenville College, Greenville, Illinois 62246
1) Free Methodist; emphasis is Holiness/Wesleyan
2) 650 students
3) $6,525
4) 95% of freshmen applicants accepted
5) 55% of entering freshmen graduate

Judson College, Elgin, Illinois 60123
1) American Baptist
2) 500 students
3) $6,600
4) 76% of freshmen applicants accepted
5) 41% of entering freshmen graduate

Trinity Christian College, Palos Heights, Illinois 60463
1) Reformed
2) 500 students
3) $6,080

4) 85% of freshmen applicants accepted
5) 60% of entering freshmen graduate

Trinity College, Deerfield, Illinois 60015
1) Evangelical Free Church
2) 600 students
3) $6,830
4) 79% of freshmen applicants accepted
5) 47% of entering freshmen graduate

Wheaton College, Wheaton, Illinois 60187
1) Interdenominational
2) 2,200 students
3) $7,728
4) 86% of freshmen applicants accepted
5) 71% of entering freshmen graduate

Bethel College, Mishawaka, Indiana 46545
1) Missionary Church
2) 550 students
3) $5,720
4) 99% of freshmen applicants accepted
5) 50% of entering freshmen graduate

Grace College, Winona Lake, Indiana 46590
1) Grace Brethren Church; one theological emphasis is dispensationalism
2) 750 students
3) $5,244
4) 93% of freshmen applicants accepted
5) 47% of entering freshmen graduate

Huntington College, Huntington, Indiana 46750
1) United Brethren in Christ
2) 500 students
3) $6,100

    4) 89% of freshmen applicants accepted
    5) 60% of entering freshmen graduate

Indiana Wesleyan University, Marion, Indiana 46952
    1) Wesleyan Church; Holiness/Wesleyan emphasis
    2) 1,100 students
    3) $6,100
    4) 95% of freshmen applicants accepted
    5) 46% of entering freshmen graduate

Taylor University, Upland, Indiana 46989
    1) Interdenominational
    2) 1,500 students
    3) $7,694
    4) 81% of freshmen applicants accepted
    5) 70% of entering freshmen graduate

Dordt College, Sioux Center, Iowa 51250
    1) Christian Reformed Church; Reformed emphasis
    2) 1,000 students
    3) $5,990
    4) 99% of freshmen applicants accepted
    5) 60% of entering freshmen graduate

Northwestern College, Orange City, Iowa 51041
    1) Reformed Church in America
    2) 850 students
    3) $6,400
    4) 98% of freshmen applicants accepted
    5) 45% of entering freshmen graduate

Mid-America Nazarene College, Olathe, Kansas 66061
    1) Church of the Nazarene; Holiness emphasis
    2) 1,000 students
    3) $4,344

Appendix

4) 100% of freshmen applicants accepted
5) 34% of entering freshmen graduate

Asbury College, Wilmore, Kentucky 40390
1) Interdenominational; Methodist-oriented; Holiness/Wesleyan emphasis
2) 1,000 students
3) $5,943
4) 78% of freshmen applicants accepted
5) 55% of entering freshmen graduate

Gordon College, Wenham, Massachusetts 01984
1) Interdenominational
2) 1,200 students
3) $8,878
4) 80% of freshmen applicants accepted
5) 50% of entering freshmen graduate

Calvin College, Grand Rapids, Michigan 49506
1) Christian Reformed Church
2) 4,100 students
3) $6,180
4) 89% of freshmen applicants accepted
5) 33% of entering freshmen graduate

Grand Rapids Baptist College, Grand Rapids, Michigan 49505
1) General Association of Regular Baptist Churches; dispensationalist; fundamentalist
2) 950 students
3) $4,150
4) 97% of freshmen applicants accepted
5) not available

Spring Arbor College, Spring Arbor, Michigan 49283
1) Free Methodist; Holiness/Wesleyan

2) 750 students
   3) $6,549
   4) 86% of freshmen applicants accepted
   5) 30% of entering freshmen graduate

Bethel College, St. Paul, Minnesota 55112
   1) Baptist General Conference
   2) 1,700 students
   3) $7,800
   4) 87% of freshmen applicants accepted
   5) 46% of entering freshmen graduate

Northwestern College, Roseville, Minnesota 55113
   1) Interdenominational
   2) 950 students
   3) $6,960
   4) 99% of freshmen applicants accepted
   5) 33% of entering freshmen graduate

Belhaven College, Jackson, Mississippi 39202
   1) Presbyterian Church (U.S.A.)
   2) 850 students
   3) $5,130
   4) 77% of freshmen applicants accepted
   5) 41% of entering freshmen graduate

Evangel College, Springfield, Missouri 65802
   1) Assemblies of God; pentecostal emphasis
   2) 1,650 students
   3) $4,508
   4) 78% of freshmen applicants accepted
   5) 40% of entering freshmen graduate

Southwest Baptist University, Bolivar, Missouri 65613
   1) Southern Baptist Convention
   2) 1,800 students
   3) $4,940

4) 60% of freshmen applicants accepted
5) not available

Houghton College, Houghton, New York 14744
1) Wesleyan Church; theological emphasis is Holiness/Wesleyan
2) 1,250 students
3) $6,874
4) 84% of freshmen applicants accepted
5) 50% of entering freshmen graduate

King's College, Briarcliff Manor, New York 10510
1) Interdenominational
2) 600 students
3) $6,747
4) 92% of freshmen applicants accepted
5) 48% of entering freshmen graduate

Nyack College, Nyack, New York 10960
1) Christian and Missionary Alliance
2) 800 students
3) $6,186
4) 95% of freshmen applicants accepted
5) 42% of entering freshmen graduate

Roberts Wesleyan College, Rochester, New York 14624
1) Free Methodist; Holiness/Wesleyan emphasis
2) 650 students
3) $6,880
4) 93% of freshmen applicants accepted
5) 58% of entering freshmen graduate

Campbell University, Buies Creek, North Carolina 27506
1) Southern Baptist Convention
2) 2,400 students
3) $5,896
4) 61% of freshmen applicants accepted

5) 65% of entering freshmen graduate

Cedarville College, Cedarville, Ohio 45314
1) General Association of Regular Baptist Churches; fundamentalist; dispensationalist
2) 1,800 students
3) $4,730
4) not available
5) not available

Cincinnati Bible College, Cincinnati, Ohio 45204
1) Churches of Christ
2) 900 students
3) $2,670
4) 98% of freshmen applicants accepted
5) not available

Malone College, Canton, Ohio 44709
1) Evangelical Friends Church
2) 1,000 students
3) $6,207
4) 92% of freshmen applicants accepted
5) 65% of entering freshmen graduate

Mount Vernon Nazarene College, Mount Vernon, Ohio 43050
1) Church of the Nazarene; Holiness emphasis
2) 1,050 students
3) $4,654
4) 90% of freshmen applicants accepted
5) 40% of entering freshmen graduate

Bartlesville Wesleyan College, Bartlesville, Oklahoma 74006
1) Wesleyan Church; Holiness emphasis
2) 500 students
3) $4,495

4) 67% of freshmen applicants accepted
5) 22% of entering freshmen graduate

Southern Nazarene University, Bethany, Oklahoma 73008
1) Church of the Nazarene; Holiness emphasis
2) 1,300 students
3) $4,190
4) 100% of freshmen applicants accepted
5) not available

Baptist Bible College, Clarks Summit, Pennsylvania 18411
1) General Association of Regular Baptist Churches; fundamentalist; dispensationalist
2) 750 students
3) $4,752
4) not available
5) not available

Eastern College, St. Davids, Pennsylvania 19087
1) American Baptist Church
2) 950 students
3) $7,530
4) 77% of freshmen applicants accepted
5) 50% of entering freshmen graduate

Geneva College, Beaver Falls, Pennsylvania 15010
1) Reformed Presbyterian Church
2) 1,225 students
3) $6,170
4) 85% of freshmen applicants accepted
5) 34% of entering freshmen graduate

Grove City College, Grove City, Pennsylvania 16127
1) Presbyterian Church (U.S.A.)
2) 2,200 students
3) $3,800

4) 51% of freshmen applicants accepted
5) not available

Messiah College, Grantham, Pennsylvania 17027
1) Brethren in Christ
2) 1,900 students
3) $6,750
4) 69% of freshmen applicants accepted
5) 62% of entering freshmen graduate

Philadelphia College of the Bible, Langhorne Manor, Pennsylvania 19047
1) Interdenominational; dispensationalist
2) 550 students
3) $5,150
4) 76% of entering freshmen accepted
5) not available

Central Wesleyan College, Central, South Carolina 29630
1) Wesleyan Church; Holiness emphasis
2) 450 students
3) $5,300
4) 93% of freshmen applicants accepted
5) 37% of entering freshmen graduate

Columbia Bible College, Columbia, South Carolina 29230
1) Interdenominational
2) 900 students
3) $4,013
4) not available
5) not available

Bryan College, Dayton, Tennessee 37321
1) Interdenominational; one theological emphasis is dispensationalism
2) 450 students
3) $4,680

Appendix

    4) 89% of freshmen applicants accepted
    5) 33% of entering freshmen graduate

Covenant College, Lookout Mountain, Tennessee 37350
    1) Presbyterian Church in America; theological emphasis is Reformed
    2) 550 students
    3) $5,890
    4) 70% of freshmen applicants accepted
    5) 55% of entering freshmen graduate

David Lipscomb University, Nashville, Tennessee 37204
    1) Churches of Christ
    2) 2,300 students
    3) $3,950
    4) not available
    5) not available

Free Will Baptist Bible College, Nashville, Tennessee 37205
    1) Free Will Baptist
    2) 425 students
    3) $2,710
    4) 98% of freshmen applicants accepted
    5) not available

King College, Bristol, Tennessee 37620
    1) Presbyterian Church (U.S.A.)
    2) 500 students
    3) $4,950
    4) 81% of freshmen applicants accepted
    5) not available

Lee College, Cleveland, Tennessee 37311
    1) Church of God (Cleveland, Tennessee)
    2) 1,200 students
    3) $3,444
    4) 99% of freshmen applicants accepted

5) 27% of entering freshmen graduate

Tennessee Temple University, Chattanooga, Tennessee, 37407
1) Independent Baptist; fundamentalist; dispensationalist
2) 2,500 students
3) $3,380
4) not available
5) not available

Trevecca Nazarene College, Nashville, Tennessee 37203
1) Church of the Nazarene; Holiness emphasis
2) 850 students
3) $4,260
4) 99% of freshmen applicants accepted
5) 49% of entering freshmen graduate

LeTourneau College, Longview, Texas 75607
1) Interdenominational
2) 800 students
3) $5,780
4) 94% of freshmen applicants accepted
5) 63% of entering freshmen graduate

Liberty University, Lynchburg, Virginia 24506
1) Independent Baptist
2) 7,000 students
3) $4,212
4) 92% of freshmen applicants accepted
5) not available

Seattle-Pacific University, Seattle, Washington 98119
1) Free Methodist; Holiness emphasis
2) 3,000 students
3) $8,061
4) 77% of freshmen applicants accepted
5) 55% of entering freshmen graduate

EVANGELICAL COLLEGES IN CANADA

Persons wishing to study at an evangelical college in Canada have a much smaller pool to select from. I provide names and addresses of five such schools. Further information may be obtained by writing the admissions director. The colleges are listed alphabetically.

King's College
Edmonton, Alberta, Canada T5H 2M1

North American Baptist College
11525—23 Avenue
Edmonton, Alberta, Canada T6J 4T3

Ontario Bible College
25 Ballyconner Court
Toronto, Ontario, Canada M2M 4B3

Redeemer College
Ancaster, Ontario, Canada L9G 3N6

Trinity Western University
7600 Glover Road
Langley, British Columbia, Canada V3A 4R9

NOTES

Chapter Two

1. This is not the place to embark on a lengthy discussion of the meaning of *evangelical*, although I do say a bit more on the subject in a later chapter. Readers wanting more information can consult the book, *Evangelicals in America* by Ronald Nash (Nashville: Abingdon Press, 1987). As for how evangelicals relate to America's large, liberal, so-called mainline denominations, see Ronald Nash, editor, *Evangelical Renewal in the Mainline Churches* (Westchester, Illinois: Crossway Books, 1987).

2. Calvinists stress God's sovereign control over all matters, while Arminians emphasize the role of human free will in salvation.

3. Dispensationalism is a way of interpreting the Bible that draws sharp distinctions between the different ways God has dealt with human beings during different periods of time. While dispensationalists usually distinguish seven such dispensations, the two most important are the Dispensation of Law (from the giving of the Mosaic Law to the beginning of the Christian Church at Pentecost) and the Dispensation of Grace (the entire Church age that will end with the Rapture of the Church). It is important, dispensationalists say, to distinguish between the quite different ways in which God dealt with the most important groups of people in those two dispensations: the nation of Israel (Law) and the Church (Grace). The indispensable handbook for dispensationalists is the Scofield Reference Bible. The most highly respected critique of dispensationalism is Oswald T. Allis, *Prophecy and the Church* (Philadelphia: Presbyterian and Reformed Publishing Co., 1945).

4. James Orr, *The Christian View of God and the World*, 7th edition (New York: Scribner, 1904), p. 20.

5. Ibid.

6. Ibid., pp. 20–21.

7. Allan Bloom, *The Closing of the American Mind* (Chicago: University of Chicago Press, 1987), p. 57.
8. Ibid., p. 58.
9. Ibid., p. 64.
10. Ibid.
11. Paul Little, *Know Why You Believe* (Downers Grove, Illinois: InterVarsity Press, 1988).

Chapter Four
1. Nothing I say in this last paragraph is intended to suggest that Christian colleges have a license to ignore such things as truth or evidence. Unfortunately, there are Christian colleges that defend Christianity and the Bible in ways that suggest shoddy scholarship. The bad job that a few such schools may do should not detract from the fact that there are sound arguments and good scholarship that support traditional Christian beliefs. Later in this book, I'll have an opportunity to identify some books that illustrate this better approach.

Chapter Five
1. It is extremely important, when considering the full range of things that Christians believe, to distinguish between essential, or central, beliefs and nonessential convictions. What I here call an essential belief is something so crucial that any rejection of the belief is tantamount to abandoning the Christian faith. Examples of essential beliefs include the belief that God exists, belief in the Trinity, belief that Jesus Christ is the incarnate Son of God, belief that Jesus' death was an atonement for human sin, and the belief that Jesus rose from the dead. As Romans 10:9–10 and other passages indicate, such beliefs are a necessary condition for anyone's being a Christian. Nonessential, or less central, beliefs include all those matters where true Christians can disagree while still remaining believers in Christ. Examples include the well-known disagreements over the nature of church government, baptism and the Lord's supper, eschatology, and so on.

Chapter Six
1. Christian College Coalition, *Consider a Christian College* (Princeton, New Jersey: Peterson's Guides, 1988), p. 11.
2. For the record, I probably ought to make it clear that in this book I am only interested in those religious colleges that have some claim to being Christian. Moreover, I have already stated that I am writing for a Protestant

audience. Therefore, I will have nothing to say about Roman Catholic colleges.

3. For more on all this, see Ronald H. Nash, *Evangelicals in America* (Nashville: Abingdon Press, 1987). For some surprising information about a resurgence of evangelical convictions in the mainline denominations, see Ronald H. Nash, editor, *Evangelical Renewal in the Mainline Churches* (Westchester, IL.: Crossway, 1987).

4. I identify some of the mainline denominational colleges that are exceptions to this rule in the next chapter.

5. James Davison Hunter, *Evangelicalism, The Coming Generation* (Chicago: University of Chicago Press, 1987), p. 178.

Chapter Seven

1. Some very brief definitions may help the reader get past this last sentence. *Eschatology* is a fancy word theologians use to refer to the doctrine of last things. The doctrine of the Second Coming of Christ belongs to the area of eschatology. A premillennialist is someone who believes that Christ's Second Coming will occur before the period of one thousand years mentioned in Revelation 20. A pretribulationist is a premillennialist who believes that a seven-year tribulation period will precede the Second Coming and that before the tribulation begins, God will remove all Christians from the world in an event called *the rapture*. Of course, many Christians accept premillennialism while regarding pretribulationism as a horrible misreading of Scripture. Other evangelicals reject both positions in favor of a different interpretation of the key texts. If any of this helps, that's fine. If you are still confused, don't worry about it. Just ignore the matter and read on.

2. See note 2 for chapter two.

3. See note 3 for chapter two.

4. Christian College Coalition, *Consider a Christian College* (Princeton, New Jersey: Peterson's Guides, 1988), p. 7.

5. Ibid.

6. Ibid., p. 11.

7. Richard Quebedeaux, *The Worldly Evangelicals* (San Francisco: Harper and Row, 1978), p. 38.

8. Carl F. H. Henry, *Evangelicals in Search of Identity* (Waco: Word Books, 1976), p. 42.

9. Quebedeaux, *Worldly Evangelicals*, p. 92.

10. Ibid., p. 93.

11. Ibid.
12. Ibid.
13. Ibid., p. 166.
14. All subsequent quotes from Ericson are taken from his editorial in the August, 1985, issue of *The Reformed Journal*, pp. 2–4.
15. For a critical analysis of many claims made by politically radical evangelicals, see Ronald Nash, *Poverty and Wealth* (Westchester, Illinois: Crossway, 1986) and Ronald Nash, *Social Justice and the Christian Church* (Grand Rapids: Baker, 1987).
16. For a discussion of the major varieties of Marxism, see Ronald Nash, *Poverty and Wealth*, chapter 9.
17. Douglas W. Frank, *Less than Conquerors: How Evangelicals Entered the Twentieth Century* (Grand Rapids: Eerdmans, 1987).
18. Richard John Neuhaus, "Christian Monisms Against the Gospel," *The Religion and Society Report*, Vol. 4, No. 11 (November, 1987), p. 3.
19. Ibid., p. 4.
20. Paul Hollander, *The Survival of the Adversary Culture* (New Brunswick, New Jersey: Transaction Books, 1988).
21. Don Feder, "What Does the Radical Left Want on Campus," *Human Events*, March 12, 1988, p. 240.

Chapter Eight

1. James Davison Hunter, *Evangelicalism, The Coming Generation* (Chicago: University of Chicago Press, 1987), p. 172.
2. Ibid.
3. Ibid.
4. Ibid., p. 14.
5. Ibid.
6. Paul Hollander, *The Survival of the Adversary Culture* (New Brunswick: Transaction Books, 1988), p. 14.
7. Hunter, *Evangelicalism*, p. 173. Hunter's mention of religious studies must be carefully qualified. His quotation occurs in a context where he is talking primarily of the liberalizing effect that study in the social sciences and humanities in Christian colleges has. Majoring in Bible and religious studies in a Christian college does have the effect he describes. But majoring in religious studies in a liberal or secular college usually has the opposite result, as Hunter well knows.
8. Ibid., pp. 175–176.
9. Ibid., pp. 177–178.

10. Ibid., p. 177.

11. My own research into this matter and others resulted in a book devoted to correcting this and dozens of other errors. See Ronald Nash, *Christianity and the Hellenistic World* (Grand Rapids: Zondervan, 1984).

12. Out-of-print books are no longer available from the publisher. Richard Bube's book is worth any effort required to track it down. Many college libraries will have it. Perhaps some local library will be able to obtain it via interlibrary loan.

Chapter Nine

1. Ronald Nash, *Faith and Reason: Searching for a Rational Faith* (Grand Rapids: Zondervan, 1988).

2. The book identified in the first note contains a thorough discussion and evaluation of Naturalism.

3. The quotations are taken from the Humanist Manifesto of 1933 as printed in *Humanist Manifestoes I and II* (Buffalo, New York: Prometheus Books, 1973), pp. 7–11.

4. For more on this, see Ronald Nash, *Poverty and Wealth: The Christian Debate Over Capitalism* (Westchester, Il.: Crossway Books, 1986).

5. James Davison Hunter, *Evangelicals, The Coming Generation* (Chicago: University of Chicago Press, 1987), p. 26.

6. For my own assent to this claim, see Ronald Nash, *Social Justice and the Christian Church* (Grand Rapids: Baker, 1987); Ronald Nash, editor, *Liberation Theology* (Grand Rapids: Baker, 1988); and Humberto Belli and Ronald Nash, editors, *Beyond Liberation Theology*, forthcoming.

7. See Emilio Nunez, *Liberation Theology* (Chicago: Moody Press, 1985) and Humberto Belli and Ronald Nash, editors, *Beyond Liberation Theology*, forthcoming.

8. See my elaboration of this claim in Ronald Nash, *Poverty and Wealth*, and in my chapters in the book, *Beyond Liberation Theology*.

FOR FURTHER READING

The following books may be helpful in assisting parents and students reach the levels of theological and intellectual concern discussed in chapter two.

Albrecht, Mark. *Reincarnation: A Christian Appraisal.* Downers Grove: InterVarsity, 1982.
Anderson, Norman. *Christianity and World Religions.* Downers Grove: InterVarsity, 1984.
Beisner, E. Calvin. *Prosperity and Poverty.* Westchester, Illinois: Crossway, 1988.
Bruce, F. F. *Jesus: Lord and Savior.* Downers Grove: InterVarsity, 1986.
———. *The New Testament Documents: Are They Reliable?* Grand Rapids: Eerdmans, 1960.
Bube, Richard. *The Human Quest.* Waco: Word, 1971.
Craig, William Lane. *Apologetics: An Introduction.* Chicago: Moody, 1984.
———. *The Son Rises: Historical Evidence for the Resurrection of Jesus.* Chicago: Moody, 1981.
De Mar, Gary. *Surviving College Successfully.* Brentwood, Tenn.: Wolgemuth & Hyatt, 1988.
Enroth, Ronald, and others. *A Guide to Cults and New Religions.* Downers Grove: InterVarsity, 1983.

Evans, C. Stephen. *Philosophy of Religion: Thinking About Faith.* Downers Grove: InterVarsity, 1985.

———. *The Quest for Faith.* Downers Grove: InterVarsity, 1986.

Green, Michael. *The Empty Cross of Jesus.* Downers Grove: InterVarsity, 1984.

Groothuis, Douglas. *Confronting the New Age.* Downers Grove: InterVarsity, 1988.

———. *Unmasking the New Age.* Downers Grove: InterVarsity, 1986.

Habermas, Gary. *The Resurrection of Jesus: An Apologetic.* Grand Rapids: Baker, 1980.

Ladd, George E. *I Believe in the Resurrection of Jesus.* Grand Rapids: Eerdmans, 1975.

Lewis, C. S. *Mere Christianity.* New York: Macmillan, 1952.

———. *Miracles.* New York: Macmillan, 1947.

———. *The Problem of Pain.* New York: Macmillan, 1962.

Little, Paul. *Know Why You Believe.* 3rd edition. Downers Grove: InterVarsity, 1988.

Milne, Bruce. *Know the Truth: A Handbook of Christian Belief.* Downers Grove: InterVarsity, 1982.

Nash, Ronald. *Christian Faith and Historical Understanding.* Grand Rapids: Zondervan, 1984.

———. *Christianity and the Hellenistic World.* Grand Rapids: Zondervan, 1984.

———. *Evangelicals in America.* Nashville: Abingdon, 1987.

———. ed. *Evangelical Renewal in the Mainline Churches.* Westchester, Illinois: Crossway, 1987.

———. *Faith and Reason: Searching for a Rational Faith.* Grand Rapids: Zondervan, 1988.

———. ed. *Liberation Theology.* Grand Rapids: Baker, 1988.

———. *Poverty and Wealth: The Christian Debate Over Capitalism.* Westchester, Illinois: Crossway, 1986.

———. ed. *Process Theology.* Grand Rapids: Baker, 1987.

———. *Social Justice and the Christian Church*. Grand Rapids: Baker, 1983.

———. *The Concept of God*. Grand Rapids: Zondervan, 1983.

———. *The Word of God and the Mind of Man*. Grand Rapids: Zondervan, 1982.

Packer, J. I. *I Want to be a Christian*. Wheaton: Tyndale, 1977.

Ramm, Bernard. *A Christian View of Science and Scripture*. Grand Rapids: Eerdmans, 1955.

Schlossberg, Herbert. *Idols for Destruction*. Nashville: Thomas Nelson, 1983.

Sire, James. *The Universe Next Door*. Downers Grove: InterVarsity, 1988.

Stott, John. *The Authentic Jesus*. Downers Grove: InterVarsity, 1986.

———. *Basic Christianity*. Downers Grove: InterVarsity, 1958.

Wenham, John. *Easter Enigma*. Grand Rapids: Zondervan, 1984.

ABOUT THE AUTHOR

Dr. Ronald Nash has more than thirty years experience in higher education. For the past twenty-five years, he has been a professor of philosophy at a large state university in the mid-South. For twenty of these same years, he also served as a university administrator. Nash has lectured at more than fifty colleges and universities in the United States and Great Britain. He is the author or editor of twenty books, including *Faith and Reason*, *Poverty and Wealth*, and *Evangelicals in America*. He also serves on his state's Advisory Board to the United States Civil Rights Commission.

COLOPHON

The typeface for the text of this book is *Goudy Old Style*. Its creator, Frederic W. Goudy, was commissioned by American Type Founders Company to design a new Roman type face. Completed in 1915 and named Goudy Old Style, it was an instant bestseller. However, its designer had sold the design outright to the foundry, so when it became evident that additional versions would be needed to complete the family, the work was done by the foundry's own designer, Morris Benton. From the original design came seven additional weights and variants, all of which sold in great quantity. However, Goudy himself received no additional compensation for them. He later recounted a visit to the foundry with a group of printers, during which the guide stopped at one of the busy casting machines and stated, "Here's where Goudy goes down to posterity, while American Type Founders Company goes down to prosperity."

Substantive Editing by Michael S. Hyatt

Copy Editing by Susan Kirby

Cover design by Kent Puckett Associates, Atlanta, Georgia

Typography by ProtoType Graphics, Inc., Nashville, Tennessee

Printed and bound by Maple-Vail Book Manufacturing Group, Manchester, Pennsylvania

Cover printing by Weber Graphics, Chicago, Illinois